| COLLINS CLASSICS COLLECTION |

POEMS FROM OTHER AGES

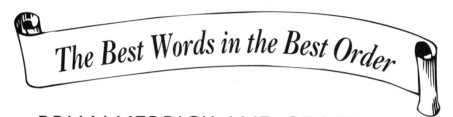

The Best Words in the Best Order

BRIAN MERRICK AND GEOFF FOX

General Editor: Geoff Fox

CollinsEducational
An imprint of HarperCollinsPublishers

ISBN 0 00 323033 3

© 1993 CollinsEducational

Brian Merrick and Geoff Fox assert the moral right to be identified as the authors of this work.

All rights reserved. No part of this publication may be reproduced, stored in a retrieval system, or transmitted in any form or by any other means, electronic, mechanical, photocopying, recording, or otherwise, without the prior permission of the Copyright owner.

First published by CollinsEducational, *an imprint of* HarperCollins *Publishers* 77-85 Fulham Palace Road, London W6 8JB.

Cover and text designed by Christie Archer

Cover illustration by Neil Dishington

Edited by Philippa Sawyer

Production by James Graves

Typeset by Wyvern Typesetting Limited

Printed by Scotprint Ltd, Musselburgh

Acknowledgements

The authors and publishers would like to thank the following for permission to reproduce illustrations:
Mansell Collection: p. 83.

Thanks are due to the following for permission to reproduce copyright material:
Macmillan London for *The Seafarer* (translated by Kevin Crossley-Holland) from *The Battle of Maldon and Other Old English Poems* edited by Bruce Mitchell; Manchester University Press for the extract from *Sir Gawain and the Green Knight* (edited and translated by W. R. J. Barron, 1974); Penguin Books for the extracts from *The General Prologue to the Canterbury Tales* (translated by Neville Coghill, 1951).

Every effort has been made to contact the holders of copyright material but if any have been inadvertently overlooked, the publishers will be pleased to make the necessary arrangements at the first opportunity.

Contents

INTRODUCTION

BALLADS

Sir Patrick Spens	*Unknown*	2
The Twa Corbies	*Unknown*	3
Edward	*Unknown*	4
Johnny Sands	*Unknown*	6
A Ballad	*A collaboration*	7
The Shepheard and the Milkmaid	*Unknown*	8
The Wraggle Taggle Gipsies	*Unknown*	9
The Ballad of Agincourt	*Michael Drayton*	10
Goody Blake and Harry Gill	*William Wordsworth*	12
Faithless Nellie Gray	*Thomas Hood*	14
Jock of Hazeldean	*Walter Scott*	15
The Song of the Lower Classes	*Ernest Jones*	16
Calling the Roll	*N.G. Shepherd*	18
The Yarn of the 'Nancy Bell'	*W.S. Gilbert*	20
Mulga Bill's Bicycle	*Banjo Paterson*	23

POEMS TO MARK AN OCCASION

David's Lament over Saul and Jonathan	*The Bible*	26
Elegy on the Death of a Mad Dog	*Oliver Goldsmith*	27
Lament for Flodden	*Jane Elliott*	28
The Burial of Sir John Moore	*Charles Wolfe*	29
The Destruction of Sennacherib	*George, Lord Byron*	30
Casabianca	*Felicia Hemans*	31
Barbara Frietchie	*John Greenleaf Whittier*	32
The Charge of the Light Brigade	*Alfred, Lord Tennyson*	34
The Railway Bridge of the Silvery Tay	*William MacGonagall*	35
To the Electors of Exeter	*Sir Edward Watkin*	37

SONNETS

Shall I compare thee to a Summer's day?	*William Shakespeare*	40
Death be not proud	*John Donne*	40
Batter my heart	*John Donne*	41

On His Blindness	*John Milton*	41
The world is too much with us	*William Wordsworth*	42
Ozymandias	*Percy Bysshe Shelley*	42
If thou must love me	*Elizabeth Barrett Browning*	43
I wish I could remember	*Christina Rossetti*	43
Remember	*Christina Rossetti*	44
Renouncement	*Alice Meynell*	44

LYRICS, ODES AND ELEGIES

The Seafarer	*Unknown*	46
My true-love hath my heart	*Philip Sidney*	49
Even such is Time	*Walter Raleigh*	49
To Daffodils	*Robert Herrick*	50
The Constant Lover	*John Suckling*	50
Death the Leveller	*James Shirley*	51
To his Coy Mistress	*Andrew Marvell*	52
The Willing Mistress	*Aphra Behn*	53
Ode on Solitude	*Alexander Pope*	54
January, 1795	*Mary Robinson*	55
The Sick Rose	*William Blake*	56
Jerusalem	*William Blake*	56
The Tyger	*William Blake*	57
The Daffodils	*William Wordsworth*	58
Lucy	*William Wordsworth*	59
She Walks in Beauty	*George, Lord Byron*	59
To Autumn	*John Keats*	60
I remember, I remember	*Thomas Hood*	61
Abou Ben Adhem	*James Henry Leigh Hunt*	62
Say not the struggle nought availeth	*Arthur Hugh Clough*	63
Stanzas	*Emily Brontë*	64
Dover Beach	*Matthew Arnold*	65
I'll tell you how the Sun rose	*Emily Dickinson*	67
I fear a Man of frugal Speech	*Emily Dickinson*	67
A Narrow Fellow in the Grass	*Emily Dickinson*	68
Pied Beauty	*Gerard Manley Hopkins*	69
Sea Love	*Charlotte Mew*	69
The Way Through the Woods	*Rudyard Kipling*	70

POEMS PUBLISHED FOR CHILDREN

One old Oxford ox opening oysters	*Unknown*	72
The Birched Schoolboy	*Unknown*	73
The Boy Serving at Table	*John Lydgate*	74

Contents

Worth Remembering	*Unknown*	75
Two Children in the Wood	*Unknown*	76
Peter Piper's Practical Principles	*Unknown*	78
Little Jack Jingle	*Unknown*	80
A Visit to the Lunatic Asylum	*Henry Sharpe Horsley*	81
Sad Effects of Gunpowder	*Unknown*	82
The Results of Stealing a Pin	*Unknown*	83
Give with Prudence	*Unknown*	83
The Umbrella	*Unknown*	84
Thoughtless Julia	*Unknown*	84
The Dreadful Story about Harriet and the Matches	*Heinrich Hoffman*	85
Dear Mother, Let me Go!	*Unknown*	87
Fear No NME	*William Martin*	88
The Blind Men and the Elephant	*John Godfrey Saxe*	89
Jabberwocky	*Lewis Carroll*	90
The Lobster Quadrille	*Lewis Carroll*	92
The Courtship of the Yonghy-Bonghy-Bò	*Edward Lear*	95
Muff Brown	*Robert Richardson*	98

NARRATIVES

Sir Gawain and the Green Knight (extract)	*Unknown*	100
Sir Gawain and the Green Knight (Modern English version)	*W. R. J. Barron*	101
The Canterbury Tales (extracts)	*Geoffrey Chaucer*	102–108
The Canterbury Tales (Modern English version)	*Neville Coghill*	103–109
Kubla Khan	*Samuel Taylor Coleridge*	110
Peter Grimes	*George Crabbe*	112
La Belle Dame Sans Merci	*John Keats*	115
The Song of Hiawatha (extract)	*Henry Wadsworth Longfellow*	116
The Sorrows of Werther	*William Makepeace Thackeray*	117
Porphyria's Lover	*Robert Browning*	118
Morte d'Arthur (extracts)	*Alfred, Lord Tennyson*	119
The Lady of Shalott	*Alfred, Lord Tennyson*	124
How They Brought the Good News from Ghent to Aix	*Robert Browning*	127
She was Poor but she was Honest	*Unknown*	129

SONGS

Adam Lay Ybounden	*Unknown*	132
I Sing of a Maiden	*Unknown*	132
A Psalm of David	*The Bible*	133
The man upright of life	*Thomas Campion*	133
Jack and Joan they think no ill	*Thomas Campion*	134
Beauty sat bathing by a spring	*Anthony Munday*	135
Since your sweet cherry lips I kissed	*Francis Davison*	135
Love in thy youth, fair maid	*Walter Porter*	136
Look on me ever	*Walter Porter*	136
Gather ye rose-buds while ye may	*Robert Herrick*	137
Cherry ripe	*Robert Herrick*	137
The Shepherd Boy's Song	*John Bunyan*	138
The Song of Master Valiant-for-Truth	*John Bunyan*	139
When icicles hang by the wall	*William Shakespeare*	139
Fear no more the heat o' the sun	*William Shakespeare*	140
Sally in our Alley	*Henry Carey*	141
The Sluggard	*Isaac Watts*	142
No riches from his scanty store	*Helen Maria Williams*	143
Ye banks and braes	*Robert Burns*	144
A red, red rose	*Robert Burns*	144
The War Song of Dinas Vawr	*Thomas Love Peacock*	145
Yes, Mary Ann	*Amelia Opie*	145
Caller Herrin'	*Carolina Nairne*	146
Sing me a song of a lad that is gone	*Robert Louis Stevenson*	147
Battle Hymn of the Republic	*Julia Ward Howe*	148
A Nightmare	*W. S. Gilbert*	149

ENDPAGE

On Prince Frederick	*Unknown*	151
The Death of Huskisson	*T. Baker*	151
On Peter Robinson	*Lord Jeffrey*	151

Index to Authors	152

INTRODUCTION

Here is humour and tragedy, slap-stick and horror, love and despair, but most importantly a wealth of insights into what it is to be human now, as well as what it was like for generations before us. These are poems which speak to men and women of all times.

We began this collection by recalling the poems we ourselves encountered at school which have left a lasting impression on us. Beyond that we have gathered together poems we have met more recently, that were published before this century and which we regard highly now. These are poems we not only enjoy, but poems we would want to share with students in the secondary school and beyond.

Brian Merrick and Geoff Fox

(opposite) 'Dante and Virgil Ascending the Mountain of Purgatory', William Blake, c. 1826

Ballads

Sir Patrick Spens

The king sits in Dumferling toune,
   Drinking the blude-reid wine:
O quhar* will I get guid sailòr,
   To sail this schip of mine

Up and spak an eldern knicht,*
   Sat at the kings richt kne:
Sir Patrick Spens is the best sailòr,
   That sails upon the se.

The king has written a braid* letter,
   And signd it wi' his hand;
And sent it to Sir Patrick Spens,
   Was walking on the sand.

The first line that Sir Patrick red,
   A loud lauch* lauched he:
The next line that Sir Patrick red,
   The teir blinded his ee.

O quha* is this has don this deid,
   This ill deid don to me;
To send me out this time o' the zeir,*
   To sail upon the se.

Mak hast, mak haste, my mirry men all,
   Our guid schip sails the morne,
O say na sae, my master deir,
   For I feir a deadlie storme.

Late late yestreen I saw the new moone
   Wi' the auld moone in hir arme;
And I feir, I feir, my deir mastèr,
   That we will com to harme.

O our Scots nobles wer richt laith
   To weet their cork-heild schoone;*
Bot lang owre a' the play wer playd,
   Thair hats they swam aboone.

O lang, lang, may thair ladies sit
   Wi' thair fans into their hand,
Or eir they se Sir Patrick Spens
   Cum sailing to the land.

O lang, lang, may the ladies stand
   Wi' thair gold kems* in their hair,
Waiting for thair ain* deir lords,
   For they'll se thame na mair.

Have owre, have owre to Aberdour,
   It's fiftie fadom deip:
And thair lies guid Sir Patrick Spens,
   Wi' the Scots lords at his feit.

Unknown

* quhar – where
* knicht – knight
* braid – plain
* lauch – laugh
* quha – who
* zeir – year
* schoone – shoes
* kems – combs
* ain – own

The Twa Corbies

As I was walking all alane
I heard twa corbies* making a mane;*
The tane unto the t'other say,
'Where sall we gang and dine today?'

'– In behint yon auld fail* dyke,
I wot there lies a new-slain Knight;
And naebody kens that he lies there,
But his hawk, his hound, and lady fair.

'His hound is to the hunting gane,
His hawk to fetch the wild-fowl hame,
His lady's ta'en another mate,
So we may mak our dinner sweet.

'Ye'll sit on his white hause-bane,*
And I'll pick out his bonnie blue een:
Wi'ae lock o' his gowden hair
We'll theek* our nest when it grows bare.

'Mony a one for him makes mane,
But nane sall ken where he is gane;
O'er his white banes, when they are bare,
The wind sall blaw for evermair.'

Unknown

* corbies – ravens
* mane – moan
* fail – turf
* hause – neck
* theek – thatch

Edward

'Why does your brand sae drop wi' blude,
    Edward, Edward?
Why does your brand sae drop wi' blude,
    And why sae sad gang ye, O?
'O I hae kill'd my hawk sae gude,
    Mither, mither;
O I hae kill'd my hawk sae gude,
    And I had nae mair but he, O.'

'Your hawk's blude was never sae red,
    Edward, Edward;
Your hawk's blude was never sae red,
    My dear son, I tell thee, O.'
'O I hae kill'd my red-roan steed,
    Mither, mither;
O I hae kill'd my red-roan steed,
    That erst was sae fair and free, O.'

'Your steed was auld, and ye hae got mair,
    Edward, Edward;
Your steed was auld, and ye hae got mair;
    Some other dule ye dree,* O.'
'O I hae kill'd my father dear,
    Mither, mither;
O I hae kill'd my father dear,
    Alas, and wae is me, O!'

'And whatten penance will ye dree for that,
    Edward, Edward?
Whatten penance will ye dree for that?
    My dear son, now tell me, O.'
'I'll set my feet in yonder boat,
    Mither, mither;
I'll set my feet in yonder boat,
    And I'll fare over the sea, O.'

* grief you suffer

'And what will ye do wi' your tow'rs and your ha',
   Edward, Edward?
And what will ye do wi' your tow'rs and your ha',
   That were sae fair to see, O?'
'I'll let them stand till they doun fa',
   Mither, mither;
I'll let them stand till they doun fa',
   For here never mair maun I be, O'

'And what will ye leave to your bairns and your wife,
   Edward, Edward?
And what will ye leave to your bairns and your wife,
   When ye gang owre the sea, O?'
'The warld's room: let them beg through life,
   Mither, mither;
The warld's room: let them beg through life;
   For them never mair will I see, O.'

'And what will ye leave to your ain mither dear,
   Edward, Edward?
And what will ye leave to your ain mither dear,
   My dear son, now tell me, O?'
'The curse of hell frac me sall ye bear,
   Mither, mither,
The curse of hell frae me sall ye bear:
   Sic counsels ye gave to me, O!'

Unknown

Johnny Sands

A MAN whose name was Johnny Sands
   Had married Betty Haigh,
And tho' she brought him gold and lands,
   She proved a terrible plague.
For, oh, she was a scolding wife,
   Full of caprice and whim,
He said that he was tired of life,
   And she was tired of him
   And she was tired of him.

Says he, then I will drown myself –
   The river runs below
Says she, pray do you silly elf,
   I wished it long ago
Says he, upon the brink I'll stand,
   Do you run down the hill
And push me in with all your might.
   Says she, my love, I will
   Says she, my love, I will.

For fear that I should courage lack
   And try to save my life,
Pray tie my hands behind my back.
   I will, replied his wife.
She tied them fast as you may think,
   And when securely done,
Now stand, she says, upon the brink,
   And I'll prepare to run,
   And I'll prepare to run.

All down the hill his loving bride,
   Now ran with all her force
To push him in – he stepped aside
   And she fell in of course
Now splashing, dashing, like a fish,
   Oh, save me, Johnny Sands,
I can't my dear, tho' much I wish,
   For you have tied my hands
   For you have tied my hands.

Unknown (17th Century)

A Ballad

'Twas when the seas were roaring
  With hollow blasts of wind;
A damsel lay deploring,
  All on a rock reclin'd.
Wide o'er the rolling billows
  She cast a wistful look;
Her head was crown'd with willows
  That tremble o'er the brook.

Twelve months are gone and over,
  And nine long tedious days.
Why didst thou, vent'rous lover,
  Why didst thou trust the seas?
Cease, cease, thou cruel ocean,
  And let my lover rest:
Ah! what's thy troubled motion
  To that within my breast?

The merchant, rob'd of pleasure,
  Sees tempests in despair;
But what's the loss of treasure
  To losing of my dear?
Should you some coast be laid on
  Where gold and di'monds grow,
You'd find a richer maiden,
  But none that loves you so.

How can they say that nature
  Has nothing made in vain;
Why then beneath the water
  Should hideous rocks remain?
No eyes the rocks discover,
  That lurk beneath the deep,
To wreck the wand'ring lover,
  And leave the maid to weep.

All melancholy lying,
  Thus wail'd she for her dear;
Repay'd each blast with sighing,
  Each billow with a tear;
When, o'er the white wave stooping,
  His floating corpse she spy'd;
Then like a lily drooping,
  She bow'd her head, and dy'd.

First appeared in a farce called The What D'ye Call It *in 1715, which Alexander Pope, John Gay, John Arbuthnot and Jonathan Swift collaborated in writing.*

The Shepheard and the Milkmaid

I'le tell you a Tale of my Love and I,
How we did often a milking goe;
And when I look't merrily, then she would cry,
   And still in her fits she would use me so.
At last I plainly did tell her my mind,
   And then she began to love me;
I ask'd her the cause of her being unkind?
   She said, It was only to prove me!

I then did give her a kiss or two,
   Which she return'd with interest still;
I thought I had now no more to do.
   But that with her I might have my will.
But she, being taught by her crafty Dad,
   Began to be cautious and wary;
And told me, When I my will had had,
   The Divell a bit I would marry.

So marry'd we were, and when it was o'er,
   I told her plain, in the Parsonage Hall,
That if she had gi'n me my will before,
   The Divell a bit I'de a marry'd at all.
She smil'd, and presently told me her mind:
   She had vow'd she'd never do more so,
Because she was cozen'd (in being too kind)
   By three or four men before so.

Unknown (17th century)

The Wraggle Taggle Gipsies

Three gipsies stood at the Castle gate,
 They sang so high, they sang so low;
The lady sate in her chamber late,
Her heart it melted away as snow.

They sang so sweet, they sang so shrill,
That fast her tears began to flow.
And she laid down her silken gown,
Her golden rings, and all her show.

She's taken off her high-heeled shoes
All made of the Spanish leather, O.
She would in the street with her bare,
 bare feet
All out in the wind and weather, O.

"O saddle to me my milk-white steed,
And go and fetch my pony, O!
That I may ride and seek my bride,
Who is gone with the wraggle taggle
 gipsies, O!"

O he rode high, and he rode low,
He rode thro' wood and copses too,
Until he came to an open field,
And there he espied his lady, O!

"What makes you leave your house and land?
Your golden treasures to forgo?
What makes you leave your new-wedded lord,
To follow the wraggle taggle gipsies, O?"

"What care I for my house and my land?
What care I for my treasure, O?
What care I for my new-wedded lord, –
I'm off with the wraggle taggle gipsies, O!"

"Last night you slept on a goose-feather bed,
With the sheet turned down so bravely, O?
But to-night you'll sleep in a cold open field,
Along with the wraggle taggle gipsies, O!"

"What care I for a goose-feather bed,
With the sheet turned down so bravely, O?
For to-night I shall sleep in a cold open field,
Along with the wraggle taggle gipsies, O!"

Unknown

The Ballad of Agincourt

Fair stood the wind for France,
When we our sails advance,
Nor now to prove our chance
   Longer will tarry;
But putting to the main,
At Caux, the mouth of Seine,
With all his martial train,
   Landed King Harry.

And taking many a fort,
Furnished in warlike sort,
Marcheth towards Agincourt
   In happy hour;
Skirmishing day by day
With those that stopped his way,
Where the French general lay
   With all his power:

Which, in his height of pride,
King Henry to deride,
His ransom to provide
   To the king sending;
Which he neglects the while
As from a nation vile,
Yet with an angry smile
   Their fall portending.

Well it thine age became,
O noble Erpingham,
Which did the signal aim
   To our hid forces!
When from a meadow by,
Like a storm suddenly,
The English archery
   Struck the French horses:

With Spanish yew so strong,
Arrows a cloth-yard long,
That like to serpents stung,
   Piercing the weather;
None from his fellow starts,
But playing manly parts,
And like true English hearts
   Stuck close together.

When down their bows they threw,
And forth their bilbos* drew,
And on the French they flew,
   Not one was tardy;
Arms were from shoulders sent,
Scalps to the teeth were rent,
Down the French peasants went;
   Our men were hardy.

This while our noble king,
His broadsword brandishing,
Down the French host did ding
   As to o'erwhelm it;
And many a deep wound lent,
His arms with blood besprent,
And many a cruel dent
   Bruisèd his helmet.

Glo'ster, that duke so good,
Next of the royal blood,
For famous England stood,
   With his brave brother;
Clarence, in steel so bright,
Though but a maiden knight,
Yet in that furious fight
   Scarce such another!

* bilbos – swords

And turning to his men,
Quoth our brave Henry then,
'Though they to one be ten,
   Be not amazèd.
Yet have we well begun,
Battles so bravely won
Have ever to the sun
   By fame been raisèd.

'And for myself,' quoth he,
'This my full rest shall be;
England ne'er mourn for me,
   Nor more esteem me.
Victor I will remain
Or on this earth lie slain;
Never shall she sustain
   Loss to redeem me.

'Poitiers and Cressy tell,
When most their pride did swell,
Under our swords they fell;
   No less our skill is
Than when our grandsire great,
Claiming the regal seat,
By many a warlike feat
   Lopped the French lilies.'

The Duke of York so dread
The eager vaward* led;
With the main Henry sped,
   Amongst his henchmen;
Excester had the rear,
A braver man not there:
O Lord, how hot they were
   On the false Frenchmen!

They now to fight are gone,
Armour on armour shone,
Drum now to drum did groan,
   To hear was wonder;
That with the cries they make
The very earth did shake,
Trumpet to trumpet spake,
   Thunder to thunder.

Warwick in blood did wade,
Oxford the foe invade,
And cruel slaughter made,
   Still as they ran up;
Suffolk his axe did ply,
Beaumont and Willoughby
Bare them right doughtily,
   Ferrers and Fanhope.

Upon Saint Crispin's Day
Fought was this noble fray,
Which fame did not delay,
   To England to carry.
O when shall Englishmen
With such acts fill a pen,
Or England breed again
   Such a King Harry?

Michael Drayton (1563–1631)

* vaward – vanguard

Goody Blake And Harry Gill

A TRUE STORY

Oh! what's the matter? what's the matter?
What is't that ails young Harry Gill?
That evermore his teeth they chatter,
Chatter, chatter, chatter still!
Of waistcoats Harry has no lack,
Good duffle grey, and flannel fine;
He has a blanket on his back,
And coats enough to smother nine.

In March, December, and in July,
'Tis all the same with Harry Gill;
The neighbours tell, and tell you truly,
His teeth they chatter, chatter still.
At night, at morning, and at noon,
'Tis all the same with Harry Gill;
Beneath the sun, beneath the moon,
His teeth they chatter, chatter still!

Young Harry was a lusty drover,
And who so stout of limb as he?
His cheeks were red as ruddy clover;
His voice was like the voice of three.
Old Goody Blake was old and poor;
Ill fed she was, and thinly clad;
And any man who passed her door
Might see how poor a hut she had.

All day she spun in her poor dwelling:
And then her three hours' work at night,
Alas! 'twas hardly worth the telling,
It would not pay for candle-light.
Remote from sheltered village-green,
On a hill's northern side she dwelt,
Where from sea-blasts the hawthorns lean,
And hoary dews are slow to melt.

By the same fire to boil their pottage,
Two poor old Dames, as I have known,
Will often live in one small cottage;
But she, poor Woman! housed alone.
'Twas well enough, when summer came,
The long, warm, lightsome summer-day,
Then at her door the canty Dame
Would sit, as any linnet, gay.

But when the ice our streams did fetter,
Oh then how her old bones would shake!
You would have said, if you had met her,
'Twas a hard time for Goody Blake.
Her evenings then were dull and dead:
Sad case it was, as you may think,
For very cold to go to bed;
And then for cold not sleep a wink.

O joy for her! whene'er in winter
The winds at night had made a rout;
And scattered many a lusty splinter
And many a rotten bough about.
Yet never had she, well or sick,
As every man who knew her says,
A pile beforehand, turf or stick,
Enough to warm her for three days.

Now, when the frost was past enduring,
And made her poor old bones to ache,
Could any thing be more alluring
Than an old hedge to Goody Blake?
And, now and then, it must be said,
When her old bones were cold and chill,
She left her fire, or left her bed,
To seek the hedge of Harry Gill.

Now Harry he had long suspected
This trespass of old Goody Blake;
And vowed that she should be detected–
That he on her would vengeance take.
And oft from his warm fire he'd go,
And to the fields his road would take;
And there, at night, in frost and snow,
He watched to seize old Goody Blake.

And once, behind a rick of barley,
Thus looking out did Harry stand:
The moon was full and shining clearly,
And crisp with frost the stubble land.
– He hears a noise – he's all awake –
Again? – on tip-toe down the hill
He softly creeps – 'tis Goody Blake;
She's at the hedge of Harry Gill!

Right glad was he when he beheld her:
Stick after stick did Goody pull:
He stood behind a bush of elder,
Till she had filled her apron full.
When with her load she turned about,
The by-way back again to take;
He started forward, with a shout,
And sprang upon poor Goody Blake.

And fiercely by the arm he took her,
And by the arm he held her fast,
And fiercely by the arm he shook her,
And cried, "I've caught you then at last!"
Then Goody, who had nothing said,
Her bundle from her lap let fall;
And, kneeling on the sticks, she prayed
To God that is the judge of all.

She prayed, her withered hand uprearing,
While Harry held her by the arm –
"God! who art never out of hearing,
O may he never more be warm!"
The cold, cold moon above her head,
Thus on her knees did Goody pray;
Young Harry heard what she had said:
And icy cold he turned away.

He went complaining all the morrow
That he was cold and very chill:
His face was gloom, his heart was sorrow,
Alas! that day for Harry Gill!
That day he wore a riding-coat,
But not a whit the warmer he:
Another was on Thursday brought,
And ere the Sabbath he had three.

'Twas all in vain, a useless matter,
And blankets were about him pinned;
Yet still his jaws and teeth they clatter,
Like a loose casement in the wind.
And Harry's flesh it fell away;
And all who see him say, 'tis plain,
That, live as long as live he may,
He never will be warm again.

No word to any man he utters,
A-bed or up, to young or old;
But ever to himself he mutters,
"Poor Harry Gill is very cold."
A-bed or up, by night or day;
His teeth they chatter, chatter still.
Now think, ye farmers all, I pray,
Of Goody Blake and Harry Gill!

William Wordsworth (1770–1850)

Faithless Nelly Gray

Ben Battle was a soldier bold,
  And used to war's alarms;
But a cannon-ball took off his legs,
  So he laid down his arms!

Now as they bore him off the field,
  Said he, 'Let others shoot,
For here I leave my second leg,
  And the Forty-second Foot!'

The army-surgeons made him limbs:
  Said he – 'They're only pegs:
But there's as wooden members quite
  As represent my legs!'

Now Ben he loved a pretty maid,
  Her name was Nelly Gray;
So he went to pay her his devours
  When he'd devoured his pay!

But when he called on Nelly Gray,
  She made him quite a scoff;
And when she saw his wooden legs
  Began to take them off!

'Oh, Nelly Gray! Oh, Nelly Gray!
  Is this your love so warm?
The love that loves a scarlet coat
  Should be more uniform!'

Said she, 'I loved a soldier once,
  For he was blithe and brave;
But I will never have a man
  With both legs in the grave!

'Before you had those timber toes,
  Your love I did allow,
But then, you know, you stand upon
  Another footing now!'

'Oh, Nelly Gray! Oh, Nelly Gray!
  For all your jeering speeches,
At duty's call, I left my legs
  In Badajos's *breaches*!'

'Why then,' said she, 'you've lost the feet
  Of legs in war's alarms,
And now you cannot wear your shoes
  Upon your feats of arms!'

'Oh, false and fickle Nelly Gray;
  I know why you refuse:–
Though I've no feet – some other man
  Is standing in my shoes!

'I wish I ne'er had seen your face;
  But, now, a long farewell!
For you will be my death – alas!
  You will not be my *Nell*!'

Now when he went from Nelly Gray,
  His heart so heavy got –
And life was such a burthen grown,
  It made him take a knot!

So round his melancholy neck,
  A rope he did entwine,
And, for his second time in life,
  Enlisted in the Line!

One end he tied around a beam,
  And then removed his pegs,
And, as his legs were off, – of course,
  He soon was off his legs!

And there he hung, till he was dead
  As any nail in town, –
For though distress had cut him up,
  It could not cut him down!

A dozen men sat on his corpse,
  To find out why he died –
And they buried Ben in four cross-roads,
  With a *stake* in his inside!

Thomas Hood (1798–1845)

Jock of Hazeldean

'Why weep ye by the tide, ladie?
    Why weep ye by the tide?
I'll wed ye to my youngest son,
    And ye shall be his bride:
And ye shall be his bride, ladie,
    Sae comely to be seen' –
But aye she loot the tears down fa'
    For Jock of Hazeldean.

'Now let this wilfu' grief be done,
    And dry that cheek so pale;
Young Frank is chief of Errington,
    And lord of Langley-dale;
His step is first in peaceful ha',
    His sword in battle keen' –
But aye she loot the tears down fa'
    For Jock of Hazeldean.

'A chain of gold ye shall not lack,
    Nor braid to bind your hair;
Nor mettled hound, nor managed hawk,
    Nor palfrey fresh and fair;
And you, the foremost of them a',
    Shall ride our forest queen' –
But aye she loot the tears down fa'
    For Jock of Hazeldean.

The kirk was deck'd at morning-tide,
    The tapers glimmer'd fair;
The priest and bridegroom wait the bride,
    And dame and knight are there.
They sought her baith by bower and ha';
    The ladie was not seen!
She's o'er the Border, and awa'
    Wi' Jock of Hazeldean.

Sir Walter Scott (1771–1832)

The Song of the Lower Classes

WE plough and sow – we're so very, very low,
   That we delve in the dirty clay,
Till we bless the plain – with the golden grain,
   And the vale with the fragrant hay,
Our place we know, – we're so very low,
   'Tis down at the landlord's feet:
We're not too low – the bread to grow,
   But too low the bread to eat.

Down, down we go, – we're so very low,
   To the hell of the deep sunk mines,
But we gather the proudest gems that glow,
   When the crown of a despot shines.
And whenever he lacks – upon our backs
   Fresh loads he deigns to lay:
We're far too low to vote the tax,
   But not too low to pay.

We're low – we're low – mere rabble, we know
   But, at our plastic power,
The mould at the lordling's feet will grow
   Into palace and church and tower.
Then prostrate fall – in the rich man's hall,
   And cringe at the rich man's door;
We're not too low to build the wall,
   But too low to tread the floor.

We're low – we're low – we're very, very low,
   Yet from our fingers glide
The silken flow – and the robes that glow
   Round the limbs of the sons of pride.
And what we get – and what we give –
   We know, and we know our share;
We're not too low the cloth to weave,
   But too low the Cloth to wear!

We're low – we're low – we're very, very low,
   And yet when the trumpets ring,
The thrust of a poor man's arm will go
   Thro' the heart of the proudest King.
We're low – we're low – our place we know,
   We're only the rank and file,
We're not too low – to kill the foe,
   But too low to touch the spoil.

Ernest Jones (1819–1869)

Calling the Roll

"Corporal Green!" the orderly cried;
   "Here!" was the answer, loud and clear,
  From the lips of a soldier standing near;
And "here!" was the word the next replied.
"Cyrus Drew!" and a silence fell;
  This time, no answer followed the call;
  Only his rear-man saw him fall,
Killed or wounded, he could not tell.

There they stood in the failing light,
   These men of battle, with grave, dark looks,
   As plain to be read as open books,
While slowly gathered the shades of night.
The fern on the slope was splashed with blood,
   And down in the corn, where the poppies grew,
   Were redder stains than the poppies knew;
And crimson-dyed was the river's flood.

For the foe had crossed from the other side,
   That day, in the face of a murderous fire
   That swept them down in its terrible ire;
And their life-blood went to color the tide.
"Herbert Cline!" At the call there came
   Two stalwart soldiers into the line,
   Bearing between them Herbert Cline,
Wounded and bleeding, to answer his name.

"Ezra Kerr!" and a voice said "here!"
   "Hiram Kerr!" but no man replied:
   They were brothers, these two; the sad wind sighed,
And a shudder crept through the corn-field near.
"Ephraim Deane!" – then a soldier spoke:
   "Deane carried our regiment's colors," he said,
   "When our ensign was shot; I left him dead,
Just after the enemy wavered and broke.

"Close to the roadside his body lies:
   I paused a moment, and gave him to drink;
   He murmured his mother's name, I think;
And death came with it and closed his eyes."
'Twas a victory – yes; but it cost us dear;
   For that company's roll, when called at night,
   Of a hundred men who went into the fight,
Numbered but twenty that answered "*here!*"

Nathaniel Graham Shepherd (1835–1896)

The Yarn of the "Nancy Bell"

'Twas on the shores that round our coast
   From Deal to Ramsgate span,
That I found alone on a piece of stone
   An elderly naval man.

His hair was weedy, his beard was long,
   And weedy and long was he,
And I heard this wight on the shore recite,
   In a singular minor key:

"Oh, I am a cook and a captain bold,
   And the mate of the *Nancy* brig,
And a bo'sun tight, and a midshipmite,
   And the crew of the captain's gig."

And he shook his fists and he tore his hair,
   Till I really felt afraid,
For I couldn't help thinking the man had been drinking,
   And so I simply said:

"Oh, elderly man, it's little I know
   Of the duties of men of the sea,
And I'll eat my hand if I understand
   However you can be.

"At once a cook, and a captain bold,
   And the mate of the *Nancy* brig,
And a bo'sun tight, and a midshipmite,
   And the crew of the captain's gig."

Then he gave a hitch to his trousers, which
   Is a trick all seamen larn,
And having got rid of a thumping quid,
   He spun this painful yarn:

"'Twas in the good ship *Nancy Bell*
   That we sailed to the Indian Sea,
And there on a reef we come to grief,
   Which has often occurred to me.

"And pretty nigh all the crew was drowned
   (There was seventy-seven o' soul),
And only ten of the *Nancy's* men
   Said 'Here!' to the muster-roll.

"There was me and the cook and the captain bold,
   And the mate of the *Nancy* brig,
And the bo'sun tight, and a midshipmite,
   And the crew of the captain's gig.

"For a month we'd neither wittles nor drink,
   Till a-hungry we did feel,
So we drawed a lot, and, accordin' shot
   The captain for our meal.

"The next lot fell to the *Nancy's* mate,
   And a delicate dish he made;
Then our appetite with the midshipmite
   We seven survivors stayed.

"And then we murdered the bo'sun tight,
   And he much resembled pig;
Then we wittled free, did the cook and me,
   On the crew of the captain's gig.

"Then only the cook and me was left,
   And the delicate question, 'Which
Of us two goes to the kettle?' arose,
   And we argued it out as sich.

"For I loved that cook as a brother, I did,
   And the cook he worshipped me;
But we'd both be blowed if we'd either be stowed
   In the other chap's hold, you see.

"'I'll be eat if you dines off me,' says Tom;
  'Yes, that,' says I, 'you'll be, –
'I'm boiled if I die, my friend,' quoth I;
  And 'Exactly so,' quoth he.

"Says he, 'Dear James, to murder me
  Were a foolish thing to do,
For don't you see that you can't cook *me*,
  While I can – and will – cook *you*!'

"So he boils the water, and takes the salt
  And the pepper in portions true
(Which he never forgot), and some chopped shalot,
  And some sage and parsley too.

"'Come here,' says he, with a proper pride,
  Which his smiling features tell,
''Twill soothing be if I let you see
  How extremely nice you'll smell.'

"And he stirred it round and round and round,
  And he sniffed at the foaming froth;
When I ups with his heels, and smothers his squeals
  In the scum of the boiling broth.

"And I eat that cook in a week or less,
  And – as I eating be
The last of his chops, why, I almost drops,
  For a wessel in sight I see!

        * * * *

"And I never larf, and I never smile,
  And I never lark nor play,
But sit and croak, and a single joke
  I have – which is to say:

"'Oh, I am a cook and a captain bold,
  And the mate of the *Nancy* brig,
And a bo'sun tight, and a midshipmite,
  And the crew of the captain's gig!'"

W.S. Gilbert (1836–1911)

Mulga Bill's Bicycle

'Twas Mulga Bill, from Eaglehawk, that caught the cycling craze;
He turned away the good old horse that served him many days;
He dressed himself in cycling clothes, resplendent to be seen;
He hurried off to town and bought a shining new machine;
And as he wheeled it through the door, with air of lordly pride,
The grinning shop assistant said, "Excuse me, can you ride?"

"See here, young man," said Mulga Bill, "from Walgett to the sea,
From Conroy's Gap to Castlereagh, there's none can ride like me.
I'm good all round at everything, as everybody knows,
Although I'm not the one to talk – I hate a man that blows.

"But riding is my special gift, my chiefest, sole delight;
Just ask a wild duck can it swim, a wild cat can it fight.
There's nothing clothed in hair or hide, or built of flesh or steel,
There's nothing walks or jumps, or runs, on axle, hoof, or wheel,
But what I'll sit, while hide will hold and girths and straps are tight;
I'll ride this here two-wheeled concern right straight away at sight."

'Twas Mulga Bill, from Eaglehawk, that sought his own abode,
That perched above the Dead Man's Creek, beside the mountain road.
He turned the cycle down the hill and mounted for the fray,
But ere he'd gone a dozen yards it bolted clean away.
It left the track, and through the trees, just like a silver streak,
It whistled down the awful slope towards the Dead Man's Creek.

It shaved a stump by half an inch, it dodged a big white-box:
The very wallaroos in fright went scrambling up the rocks,
The wombats hiding in their caves dug deeper underground,
But Mulga Bill, as white as chalk, sat tight to every bound.
It struck a stone and gave a spring that cleared a fallen tree,
It raced beside a precipice as close as close could be;
And then, as Mulga Bill let out one last despairing shriek,
It made a leap of twenty feet into the Dead Man's Creek.

Ballads

'Twas Mulga Bill, from Eaglehawk, that slowly swam ashore:
He said, "I've had some narrer shaves and lively rides before;
I've rode a wild bull round a yard to win a five-pound bet,
But this was sure the derndest ride that I've encountered yet.
I'll give that two-wheeled outlaw best; it's shaken all my nerve
To feel it whistle through the air and plunge and buck and swerve,
It's safe at rest in Dead Man's Creek – we'll leave it lying still;
A horse's back is good enough henceforth for Mulga Bill."

Banjo Paterson (1864 – 1941)

(opposite) Detail from 'The March to Finchley', William Hogarth, 1749–50

Poems to Mark an Occasion

David's Lament over Saul and Jonathan

And David lamented with this lamentation over Saul and over Jonathan his son:

The beauty of Israel is slain upon thy high places: how are the mighty fallen!

Tell it not in Gath, publish it not in the streets of Askelon lest the daughters of the Philistines rejoice, lest the daughters of the uncircumcised triumph.

Ye mountains of Gilboa, let there be no dew, neither let there be rain, upon you, nor fields of offerings: for there the shield of the mighty is vilely cast away, the shield of Saul, as though he had not been anointed with oil.

From the blood of the slain, from the fat of the mighty, the bow of Jonathan turned not back, and the sword of Saul returned not empty.

Saul and Jonathan were lovely and pleasant in their lives, and in their death they were not divided: they were swifter than eagles, they were stronger than lions.

Ye daughters of Israel, weep over Saul, who clothed you in scarlet, with other delights, who put on ornaments of gold upon your apparel.

How are the mighty fallen in the midst of the battle! O Jonathan, thou wast slain in thine high places.

I am distressed for thee, my brother Jonathan: very pleasant hast thou been unto me: thy love to me was wonderful, passing the love of women.

How are the mighty fallen, and the weapons of war perished!

From The Second Book of Samuel, *Chapter 1, verses 17–27 (Authorised King James Version)*

Elegy on the Death of a Mad Dog

Good people all, of every sort,
　Give ear unto my song;
And if you find it wondrous short,
　It cannot hold you long.

In Islington there was a man,
　Of whom the world might say,
That still a godly race he ran,
　Whene'er he went to pray.

A kind and gentle heart he had,
　To comfort friends and foes;
The naked every day he clad,
　When he put on his clothes.

And in that town a dog was found,
　As many dogs there be,
Both mongrel, puppy, whelp, and hound,
　And curs of low degree.

This dog and man at first were friends;
　But when a pique began,
The dog, to gain some private ends,
　Went mad and bit the man.

Around from all the neighbouring streets
　The wondering neighbours ran,
And swore the dog had lost his wits,
　To bite so good a man.

The wound it seemed both sore and sad
　To every Christian eye;
And while they swore the dog was mad,
　They swore the man would die.

But soon a wonder came to light,
　That showed the rogues they lied:
The man recovered of the bite –
　The dog it was that died.

Oliver Goldsmith (1730 – 1774)

Lament for Flodden

I've heard them lilting at our ewe-milking,
Lasses a' lilting* before dawn o' day;
But now they are moaning on ilka green loaning* –
   The Flowers of the Forest are a' wede away.

At bughts,* in the morning, nae blythe lads are scorning,
   Lasses are lonely and dowie* and wae;
Nae daffin', nae gabbin', but sighing and sabbing,
   Ilk ane lifts her leglin and hies her away.

In har'st, at the shearing, nae youths now are jeering,
   Bandsters are lyart,* and runkled, and gray;
At fair or at preaching, nae wooing, nae fleeching –
   The Flowers of the Forest are a' wede away.

At e'en, in the gloaming, nae younkers are roaming
   'Bout stacks wi' the lasses at bogle* to play;
But ilk ane sits drearie, lamenting her dearie –
   The Flowers of the Forest are weded away.

Dool* and wae for the order, sent our lads to the Border!
   The English, for ance, by guile wan the day;
The Flowers of the Forest, that fought aye the foremost,
   The prime of our land, are cauld in the clay.

We'll hear nae mair lilting at the ewe-milking
   Women and bairns are heartless and wae;
Sighing and moaning on ilka green loaning –
   The Flowers of the Forest are a' wede away.

Jane Elliott (1727 – 1805)

* lilting – singing
* loaning – lane
* bughts – time to collect the sheep for milking
* dowie – worn with grief
* lyart – old
* bogle – hobgoblins
* dool – sorrow

Poems to Mark an Occasion

The Burial of Sir John Moore

Not a drum was heard, not a funeral note,
   As his corse to the ramparts we hurried;
Not a soldier discharged his farewell shot
   O'er the grave where our hero we buried.

We buried him darkly, at dead of night,
   The sods with our bayonets turning,
By the struggling moonbeam's misty light,
   And the lantern dimly burning.

No useless coffin enclosed his breast,
   Not in sheet nor in shroud we wound him;
But he lay like a warrior taking his rest,
   With his martial cloak around him.

Few and short were the prayers we said,
   And we spoke not a word of sorrow;
But we steadfastly gazed on the face that was dead,
   And we bitterly thought of the morrow.

We thought as we hollow'd his narrow bed,
   And smoothed down his lonely pillow,
That the foe and the stranger would tread o'er his head,
   And we far away on the billow!

Lightly they'll talk of the spirit that's gone,
   And o'er his cold ashes upbraid him;
But little he'll reck if they let him sleep on,
   In the grave where a Briton has laid him.

But half of our heavy task was done,
   When the clock struck the hour for retiring,
And we heard the distant and random gun
   That the foe was sullenly firing.

Slowly and sadly we laid him down,
   From the field of his fame fresh and gory;
We carved not a line, and we raised not a stone,
   But we left him alone in his glory.

Charles Wolfe (1791–1823)

The Destruction of Sennacherib

The Assyrian came down like the wolf on the fold,
And his cohorts were gleaming in purple and gold;
And the sheen of their spears was like stars on the sea,
When the blue wave rolls nightly on deep Galilee.

Like the leaves of the forest when summer is green,
That host with their banners at sunset were seen;
Like the leaves of the forest when autumn hath blown,
That host on the morrow lay withered and strown.

For the Angel of Death spread his wings on the blast,
And breathed on the face of the foe as he passed;
And the eyes of the sleepers waxed deadly and chill,
And their hearts but once heaved, and for ever grew still!

And there lay the steed with his nostril all wide,
But through it there rolled not the breath of his pride;
And the foam of his gasping lay white on the turf,
And cold as the spray of the rock-beating surf.

And there lay the rider distorted and pale,
With the dew on his brow, and the rust on his mail;
And the tents were all silent, the banners alone,
The lances unlifted, the trumpet unblown.

And the widows of Ashur are loud in their wail,
And the idols are broke in the temple of Baal;
And the might of the Gentile, unsmote by the sword,
Hath melted like snow in the glance of the Lord!

George, Lord Byron (1788–1824)

Casabianca

The boy stood on the burning deck
   Whence all but he had fled;
The flame that lit the battle's wreck
   Shone round him o'er the dead.

Yet beautiful and bright he stood,
   As born to rule the storm;
A creature of heroic blood,
   A proud, though childlike form.

The flames roll'd on – he would not go
   Without his father's word;
That father, faint in death below,
   His voice no longer heard.

He call'd aloud – "Say, father, say
   If yet my task is done!"
He knew not that the chieftain lay
   Unconscious of his son.

"Speak, father!" once again he cried,
   "If I may yet be gone!"
And but the booming shots replied,
   And fast the flames roll'd on.

Upon his brow he felt their breath,
   And in his waving hair,
And looked from that lone post of death,
   In still yet brave despair;

And shouted but once more aloud,
   "My father, must I stay?"
While o'er him fast, through sail and shroud
   The wreathing fires made way.

They wrapt the ship in splendour wild,
   They caught the flag on high,
And stream'd above the gallant child,
   Like banners in the sky.

There came a burst of thunder sound –
   The boy – oh! where was he?
Ask of the winds that far around
   With fragments strewed the sea! –

With mast, and helm, and pennon fair,
   That well had borne their part;
But the noblest thing which perished there
   Was that young faithful heart.

Felicia Hemans (1793–1835)

Barbara Frietchie

Up from the meadows rich with corn,
Clear in the cool September morn,
The clustered spires of Frederick stand
Green-walled by the hills of Maryland.
Round and about them orchards sweep,
Apple and peach tree fruited deep,
Fair as a garden of the Lord,
To the eyes of the famished rebel horde,
On that pleasant morn of the early fall
When Lee marched over the mountain-wall;
Over the mountains winding down,
Horse and foot, into Frederick town.

Forty flags with their silver stars,
Forty flags with their crimson bars,
Flapped in the morning wind: the sun
Of noon looked down, and saw not one.
Up rose old Barbara Frietchie then,
Bowed with her fourscore years and ten;
Bravest of all in Frederick town,
She took up the flag the men hauled down;
In her attic window the staff she set,
To show that one heart was loyal yet.

Up the street came the rebel tread,
Stonewall Jackson riding ahead.
Under his slouched hat left and right
He glanced; the old flag met his sight.
'Halt!' – the dust-brown ranks stood fast.
'Fire!' – out blazed the rifle-blast.
It shivered the window, pane and sash;
It rent the banner with seam and gash.
Quick, as it fell, from the broken staff
Dame Barbara snatched the silken scarf;
She leaned far out on the window-sill,
And shook it forth with a royal will.
'Shoot, if you must, this old gray head,
But spare your country's flag,' she said.

A shade of sadness, a blush of shame,
Over the face of the leader came;
The nobler nature within him stirred
To life at that woman's deed and word;
'Who touches a hair of yon gray head
Dies like a dog! March on!' he said.
All day long through Frederick street
Sounded the tread of marching feet:
All day long that free flag tost
Over the heads of the rebel host.
Ever its torn folds rose and fell
On the loyal winds that loved it well;
And through the hill-gaps sunset light
Shone over it with a warm good-night.

Barbara Frietchie's work is o'er,
And the Rebel rides on his raids no more.
Honour to her! and let a tear
Fall, for her sake, on Stonewall's bier.
Over Barbara Frietchie's grave,
Flag of Freedom and Union, wave!
Peace and order and beauty draw
Round thy symbol of light and law;
And ever the stars above look down
On thy stars below in Frederick town!

John Greenleaf Whittier (1807–1892)

The Charge of the Light Brigade

Half a league, half a league,
Half a league onward,
All in the valley of Death
   Rode the six hundred.
'Forward, the Light Brigade!
Charge for the guns!' he said:
Into the valley of Death
   Rode the six hundred.

'Forward, the Light Brigade!'
Was there a man dismay'd?
Not tho' the soldier knew
   Someone had blunder'd:
Theirs not to make reply,
Theirs not to reason why,
Theirs but to do and die:
Into the valley of Death
   Rode the six hundred.

Cannon to right of them,
Cannon to left of them,
Cannon in front of them
   Volley'd and thunder'd;
Storm'd at with shot and shell,
Boldly they rode and well,
Into the jaws of Death,
Into the mouth of Hell
   Rode the six hundred.

Flash'd all their sabres bare,
Flash'd as they turn'd in air,
Sabring the gunners there,
Charging an army, while
   All the world wonder'd:
Plunged in the battery-smoke
Right thro' the line they broke;
Cossack and Russian
Reel'd from the sabre-stroke
Shatter'd and sunder'd.
Then they rode back, but not,
   Not the six hundred.

Cannon to right of them,
Cannon to left of them,
Cannon behind them
   Volley'd and thunder'd;
Storm'd at with shot and shell,
While horse and hero fell,
They that had fought so well
Came thro' the jaws of Death,
Back from the mouth of Hell,
All that was left of them,
   Left of six hundred.

When can their glory fade?
O the wild charge they made!
   All the world wonder'd.
Honour the charge they made!
Honour the Light Brigade,
   Noble six hundred!

Alfred, Lord Tennyson (1809–1892)

The Railway Bridge of the Silvery Tay

Beautiful Railway Bridge of the Silvery Tay!
With your numerous arches and pillars in so grand array,
And your central girders, which seem to the eye
To be almost towering to the sky.
The greatest wonder of the day,
And a great beautification to the River Tay,
Most beautiful to be seen,
Near by Dundee and the Magdalen Green.

Beautiful Railway Bridge of the Silvery Tay!
That has caused the Emperor of Brazil to leave
His home far away, *incognito* in his dress,
And view thee ere he passed along *en route* to Inverness.

Beautiful Railway Bridge of the Silvery Tay!
The longest of the present day
That has ever crossed o'er a tidal river stream,
Most gigantic to be seen,
Near by Dundee and the Magdalen Green.

Beautiful Railway Bridge of the Silvery Tay!
Which will cause great rejoicing on the opening day,
And hundreds of people will come from far away,
Also the Queen, most gorgeous to be seen,
Near by Dundee and the Magdalen Green.

Beautiful Railway Bridge of the Silvery Tay!
And prosperity to Provost Cox, who has given
Thirty thousand pounds and upwards away
In helping to erect the Bridge of the Tay,
Most handsome to be seen,
Near by Dundee and the Magdalen Green.

Beautiful Railway Bridge of the Silvery Tay!
I hope that God will protect all passengers
By night and by day,
And that no accident will befall them while crossing
The Bridge of the Silvery Tay,
For that would be most awful to be seen
Near by Dundee and the Magdalen Green.

Beautiful Railway Bridge of the Silvery Tay!
And prosperity to Messrs Bouche and Grothe,
The famous engineers of the present day,
Who have succeeded in erecting the Railway
Bridge of the Silvery Tay,
Which stands unequalled to be seen
Near by Dundee and the Magdalen Green.

William MacGonagall (1830–1902)

To the Electors of Exeter

S ilver, copper, brass in plenty,
I n my pockets mix with gold;
R ailway Shares enough for twenty,
E ndless wealth and power untold.
D ividends at all the quarters,
W ondering Clerks my Agents pay;
A rtisans and Guards and Porters,
R ailways three my word obey.
D oubt not I can help you greatly,
W ork for thousands I can bring,
A nd with Parks and Mansions stately,
T ry to prove a 'Railway King'.
K now that I am now Director,
I n the Chair of Railways three,
N ever was so great Protector,
K ing or Kaiser, Pope, as me.
N ow's your chance, my wise Elector,
T ake me for your new M.P.

Sir Edward W. Watkin (1873)

(opposite) 'Jane Burden as Queen Guenevere', Dante Gabriel Rossetti, 1858

SONNETS

'Shall I compare thee to a Summer's day?'

Shall I compare thee to a Summer's day?
Thou art more lovely and more temperate:
Rough winds do shake the darling buds of May,
And Summer's lease hath all too short a date:
Sometime too hot the eye of heaven shines,
And often is his gold complexion dimm'd,
And every fair from fair sometime declines,
By chance, or nature's changing course untrimm'd:
But thy eternal Summer shall not fade,
Nor lose possession of that fair thou ow'st,
Nor shall Death brag thou wander'st in his shade,
When in eternal lines to time thou grow'st:
    So long as men can breathe or eyes can see,
    So long lives this, and this gives life to thee.

William Shakespeare (1564–1616)

'Death be not proud'

Death be not proud, though some have called thee
Mighty and dreadfull, for, thou art not soe,
For, those, whom thou think'st, thou dost overthrow,
Die not, poore death, nor yet canst thou kill mee.
From rest and sleepe, which but thy pictures bee,
Much pleasure, then from thee, much more must flow,
And soonest our best men with thee doe goe,
Rest of their bones, and soules deliverie.
Thou art slave to Fate, Chance, kings, and desperate men,
And dost with poyson, warre, and sicknesse dwell,
And poppie, or charmes can make us sleepe as well,
And better then thy stroake; why swell'st thou then?
One short sleepe past, wee wake eternally,
And death shall be no more; death, thou shalt die.

John Donne (1573–1631)

'Batter my heart'

BATTER my heart, three person'd God; for, you
As yet but knocke, breathe, shine, and seeke to mend;
That I may rise, and stand, o'erthrow mee, and bend
Your force, to breake, blowe, burn and make me new.
I, like an usurpt towne, to another due,
Labour to admit you, but Oh, to no end,
Reason your viceroy in mee, mee should defend,
But is captiv'd, and proves weake or untrue.
Yet dearely I love you, and would be loved faine,
But am betroth'd unto your enemie:
Divorce mee, untie, or breake that knot againe,
Take mee to you, imprison mee, for I
Except you enthrall mee, never shall be free,
Nor ever chast, except you ravish mee.

John Donne

On His Blindness

WHEN I consider how my light is spent,
  Ere half my days, in this dark world and wide,
  And that one talent which is death to hide,
  Lodg'd with me useless, though my soul more bent
To serve therewith my Maker, and present
  My true account, lest He returning chide,
  Doth God exact day-labour, light denied,
  I fondly ask; but patience to prevent
That murmur, soon replies, God doth not need
  Either man's work or His own gifts; who best
  Bear His mild yoke, they serve Him best. His state
Is kingly. Thousands at His bidding speed
  And post o'er land and ocean without rest;
  They also serve who only stand and wait.

John Milton (1608–1674)

'The world is too much with us'

The world is too much with us; late and soon,
  Getting and spending, we lay waste our powers:
Little we see in Nature that is ours;
We have given our hearts away, a sordid boon!
This Sea that bares her bosom to the moon;
The winds that will be howling at all hours,
And are up-gathered now like sleeping flowers;
For this, for everything, we are out of tune;
It moves us not. – Great God! I'd rather be
A Pagan suckled in a creed outworn;
So might I, standing on this pleasant lea,
Have glimpses that would make me less forlorn;
Have sight of Proteus rising from the sea;
Or hear old Triton blow his wreathèd horn.

William Wordsworth (1770–1850)

Ozymandias

I met a traveller from an antique land
  Who said: Two vast and trunkless legs of stone
Stand in the desert. Near them, on the sand,
Half sunk, a shattered visage lies, whose frown,
And wrinkled lip, and sneer of cold command,
Tell that its sculptor well those passions read
Which yet survive (stamped on these lifeless things),
The hand that mocked them and the heart that fed;
And on the pedestal these words appear:
'My name is Ozymandias, king of kings;
Look on my works, ye Mighty, and despair!'
Nothing beside remains. Round the decay
Of that colossal wreck, boundless and bare,
The lone and level sands stretch far away.

Percy Bysshe Shelley (1792–1822)

'If thou must love me'

If thou must love me, let it be for nought
Except for love's sake only. Do not say
'I love her for her smile – her look – her way
Of speaking gently – for a trick of thought
That falls in well with mine, and certes brought
A sense of pleasant ease on such a day –
For these things in themselves, Beloved, may
Be changed, or change for thee – and love, so wrought,
May be unwrought so. Neither love me for
Thine own dear pity's wiping my cheeks dry –
A creature might forget to weep, who bore
The comfort long, and lose thy love thereby!
But love me for love's sake, that evermore
Thou mayst love on, through love's eternity.

Elizabeth Barrett Browning (1806–1861)

'I wish I could remember'

I wish I could remember that first day,
First hour, first moment of your meeting me,
If bright or dim the season, it might be
Summer or Winter for aught I can say;
So unrecorded did it slip away,
So blind was I to see and to foresee,
So dull to mark the budding of my tree
That would not blossom yet for many a May.
If only I could recollect it, such
A day of days! I let it come and go
As traceless as a thaw of bygone snow;
It seemed to mean so little, meant so much;
If only now I could recall that touch,
First touch of hand in hand – Did one but know!

Christina Rossetti (1830–1894)

Remember

Remember me when I am gone away,
 Gone far away into the silent land;
When you can no more hold me by the hand,
Nor I half turn to go yet turning stay.
Remember me when no more day by day
You tell me of our future that you plann'd:
Only remember me; you understand
It will be late to counsel then or pray.
Yet if you should forget me for a while
And afterwards remember, do not grieve:
For if the darkness and corruption leave
A vestige of the thoughts that once I had,
Better by far you should forget and smile
Than that you should remember and be sad.

Christina Rossetti

Renouncement

I must not think of thee; and, tired yet strong,
 I shun the thought that lurks in all delight –
   The love of thee – and in the blue Heaven's height,
And in the sweetest passage of a song.
O just beyond the fairest thoughts that throng
   This breast, the thought of thee waits hidden yet bright;
   But it must never, never come in sight;
I must stop short of thee the whole day long.

But when sleep comes to close each difficult day,
   When night gives pause to the long watch I keep,
   And all my bonds I needs must loose apart,
Must doff my will as raiment laid away, –
   With the first dream that comes with the first sleep
   I run, I run, I am gather'd to thy heart.

Alice Meynell (1847–1922)

(opposite) 'A Willow Beside Water, a Church Beyond', John Constable, 1832

Lyrics, Odes and Elegies

The Seafarer

I can sing a true song about myself,
Tell of my travels, of many hard times
Toiling day after day; I can describe
How I have harboured bitter sorrow in my heart
And often learned that ships are homes of sadness.
Wild were the waves when I took my turn,
The arduous night-watch, standing at the prow
While the boat tossed near the rocks. My feet
Were tortured by frost, fettered
In frozen chains; fierce anguish clutched
At my heart; passionate longings maddened
The mind of the sea-weary man. Prosperous men,
Living on land, do not begin to understand
How I, careworn and cut off from my kinsmen,
Have as an exile endured the winter
On the icy sea . . . .
Icicles hung round me; hail showers flew.
The only sound there, was of the sea booming –
The ice-cold wave – and at times the song of the swan.
The cry of the gannet was all my gladness,
The call of the curlew, not the laughter of men,
The mewing gull, not the sweetness of mead.
There, storms echoed off the rocky cliffs; the icy-feathered tern
Answered them; and often the eagle,
Dewy-winged, screeched overhead. No protector
Could console the cheerless man.

He who is accustomed to the comforts of life
And, proud and flushed with wine, suffers
Little hardship living in the city,
Will never know how I, heavy with weariness,
Have often had to make the ocean paths my home.
The night-shadow grew long, it snowed from the north,
Frost fettered the earth; hail, coldest of grain,
Battered the ground. But now my blood
Is stirred that I should make trial
Of the mountainous streams, the tossing salt waves;

My heart's longings always urge me
To undertake a journey, to visit the country
Of a foreign people far across the sea.
On earth there is no man so self-assured,
So generous with his gifts or so gallant in his youth,
So daring in his deeds or with such a gracious lord,
That he harbours no fears about his seafaring
As to what Almighty God will ordain for him.
He thinks not of the harp nor of receiving rings,
Not of rapture in a woman nor of any worldly joy,
But only of the rolling of the waves;
The seafarer will always feel longings.
The groves burst with blossom, towns become fair,
Meadows are beautiful once more, the whole world revives;
All these things urge the eager man
To set out on a journey over the salt streams.
And the cuckoo, too, harbinger of summer, sings
A mournful song, boding bitter sorrow
To the heart. Prosperous men know not
What hardship is endured by those
Who tread the paths of exile to the ends of the world.

Wherefore my heart leaps within me,
My mind roves with the waves
Over the whale's domain, it wanders far and wide
Across the face of the earth, returns again to me
Eager and unsatisfied; the solitary bird screams,
Irresistible, urging my heart to the whale's way
Over the stretch of the sea.
                              So it is that the joys
Of the Lord inspire me more than this dead life,
Ephemeral here on earth. I have no faith
That the splendours of this earth will survive for ever.
There are three things which, until one
Occurs, are always unpredictable:
Illness or age or death in battle
Can deprive a doomed man of his life.
Wherefore each man should strive, before he leaves
This world, to win the praise of those living
After him. The best of posthumous fame
Is to achieve great deeds on earth
Against the malice of the fiends, against the devil,
So that the children of men may honour a man's name

And his fame at last may live with the angels
For ever and ever, in the joy of life eternal
Amongst the heavenly host.
                          Days of great glory
In the kingdom of earth are gone forever;
Kings and emperors and gold-giving lords
Are no longer as they used to be –
Once they wrought deeds of greatest renown,
Lived in most lordly splendour;
Such excellence proved ephemeral, those joys have passed
   away;
Weaklings thrive and hold sway in the world,
Enjoy it only through their own labours; all honour is laid
   low;
The earth's flower ages and withers
As now does every man throughout this middle-world:
Old age grasps his hand, his face grows pale,
Grey-haired he mourns; he knows that his former friends,
The sons of princes, have been placed in the earth.
Then, when he dies, his lifeless body
Cannot taste sweetness, feel the sharpness of pain,
Lift a hand or be lost in reveries of the mind.
Though a brother may bury his kinsman
Amongst the dead, strew his grave with gold
And the many treasures he wished to take with him,
The shining gold which a man stores on earth
Is of no assistance to his sinful soul
Confronted at the last by God's wrath.

Great is the fear of God; through Him the world turns.
He created the mighty plains,
The face of the earth and the sky above.
Foolish is he who fears not his Lord: death will find him
   unprepared.
Blessed is the humble man: he will find mercy in Heaven.
God gave man a soul to have faith in His great strength.

Unknown (Translated from Anglo-Saxon into
modern English by Kevin Crossley-Holland)

'My true-love hath my heart'

My true-love hath my heart, and I have his,
By just exchange one for another given:
I hold his dear, and mine he cannot miss,
There never was a better bargain driven:
   My true-love hath my heart, and I have his.

His heart in me keeps him and me in one,
My heart in him his thoughts and senses guides:
He loves my heart, for once it was his own,
I cherish his because in me it bides:
   My true-love hath my heart, and I have his.

Philip Sidney (1554–1586)

'Even such is Time'

Even such is Time, that takes in trust
Our youth, our joys, our all we have,
And pays us but with earth and dust;
   Who, in the dark and silent grave,
When we have wandered all our ways,
Shuts up the story of our days;
But from this earth, this grave, this dust,
My God shall raise me up, I trust.

Walter Raleigh (1552–1618)
(Found in his Bible after his death)

To Daffodils

Fair Daffodils, we weep to see
  You haste away so soon;
As yet the early rising sun
  Has not attained his noon.
    Stay, stay,
  Until the hasting day
    Has run
  But to the even-song;
And, having prayed together, we
  Will go with you along.

We have short time to stay, as you,
  We have as short a spring;
As quick a growth to meet decay,
  As you, or anything.
    We die
  As your hours do, and dry
    Away,
  Like to the summer's rain;
Or as the pearls of morning's dew,
  Ne'er to be found again.

Robert Herrick (1591–1674)

The Constant Lover

Out upon it! I have lov'd
  Three whole days together;
And am like to love three more,
  If it prove fair weather.

Time shall moult away his wings,
  Ere he shall discover
In the whole wide world again
  Such a constant lover.

But the spite on't is, no praise
  Is due at all to me:
Love with me had made no stays,
  Had it any been but she.

Had it any been but she,
  And that very face,
There had been at least ere this
  A dozen dozen in her place.

John Suckling (1609–1642)

Death the Leveller

The glories of our blood and state
  Are shadows, not substantial things;
There is no armour against Fate;
  Death lays his icy hand on kings:
    Sceptre and Crown
    Must tumble down,
And in the dust be equal made
With the poor crooked scythe and spade.

Some men with swords may reap the field,
  And plant fresh laurels where they kill:
But their strong nerves at last must yield;
  They tame but one another still:
    Early or late
    They stoop to fate,
And must give up their murmuring breath
When they, pale captives, creep to death.

The garlands wither on your brow;
  Then boast no more your mighty deeds!
Upon Death's purple altar now
  See where the victor-victim bleeds.
    Your heads must come
    To the cold tomb;
Only the actions of the just
Smell sweet, and blossom in their dust.

James Shirley (1596–1666)

To his Coy Mistress

Had we but world enough, and time,
This coyness, Lady, were no crime,
We would sit down and think which way
To walk and pass our long love's day.
Thou by the Indian Ganges' side
Shouldst rubies find; I by the tide
Of Humber would complain. I would
Love you ten years before the Flood,
And you should, if you please, refuse
Till the conversion of the Jews.
My vegetable love should grow
Vaster than empires, and more slow;
An hundred years should go to praise
Thine eyes, and on thy forehead gaze,
Two hundred to adore each breast,
But thirty thousand to the rest;
An age at least to every part,
And the last age should show your heart.
For, Lady, you deserve this state,
Nor would I love at lower rate.

But at my back I always hear
Time's wingèd chariot hurrying near;
And yonder all before us lie
Deserts of vast eternity.
Thy beauty shall no more be found,
Nor, in thy marble vault shall sound
My echoing song; then worms shall try
That long preserved virginity,
And your quaint honour turn to dust,
And into ashes all my lust:
The grave's a fine and private place,
But none, I think, do there embrace.

Now therefore, while the youthful hue
Sits on thy skin like morning dew,
And while thy willing soul transpires
At every pore with instant fires,
Now let us sport us while we may,
And now, like amorous birds of prey,
Rather at once our time devour
Than languish in his slow-chapt power.
Let us roll all our strength and all
Our sweetness up into one ball,
And tear our pleasures with rough strife
Through the iron gates of life.
Thus, though we cannot make our sun
Stand still, yet we will make him run.

Andrew Marvell (1621–1678)

The Willing Mistress

Amyntas led me to a grove
 Where all the trees did shade us;
The sun itself though it had strove
 It could not have betrayed us.
The place secured from human eyes
 No other fear allows,
But when the winds that gently rise
 Do kiss the yielding boughs.

Down there we sat upon the moss,
 And did begin to play
A thousand amorous tricks, to pass
 The heat of all the day.
A many kisses he did give,
 And I returned the same,
Which made me willing to receive
 That which I dare not name.

His charming eyes no aid required
 To tell their softening tale;
On her that was already fired
 'Twas easy to prevail.
He did but kiss and clasp me round,
 Whilst those his thoughts exprest;
And laid me gently on the ground:
 Ah, who can guess the rest?

Aphra Behn (1640–1689)

Ode on Solitude

Happy the man, whose wish and care
   A few paternal acres bound,
Content to breathe his native air,
               In his own ground.

Whose herds with milk, whose fields with bread,
   Whose flocks supply him with attire,
Whose trees in summer yield him shade,
               In winter fire.

Blest, who can unconcern'dly find
   Hours, days, and years slide soft away,
In health of body, peace of mind,
               Quiet by day,

Sound sleep by night; study and ease,
   Together mixt; sweet recreation;
And innocence, which most does please
              With meditation.

Thus let me live, unseen, unknown,
   Thus unlamented let me die,
Steal from the world, and not a stone
              Tell where I lie.

Alexander Pope (1688–1744)

January, 1795

Pavement slippery, people sneezing,
Lords in ermine, beggars freezing;
Titled gluttons dainties carving,
Genius in a garret starving.

Lofty mansions, warm and spacious;
Courtiers cringing and voracious;
Misers scarce the wretched heeding;
Gallant soldiers fighting, bleeding.

Wives who laugh at passive spouses;
Theatres, and meeting-houses;
Balls, where simpering misses languish;
Hospitals, and groans of anguish.

Arts and sciences bewailing;
Commerce drooping, credit failing;
Placemen mocking subjects loyal;
Separations, weddings royal.

Authors who can't earn a dinner;
Many a subtle rogue a winner;
Fugitives for shelter seeking;
Misers hoarding, tradesmen breaking.

Taste and talents quite deserted;
All the laws of truth perverted;
Arrogance o'er merit soaring;
Merit silently deploring.

Ladies gambling night and morning;
Fools the works of genius scorning;
Ancient dames for girls mistaken,
Youthful damsels quite forsaken.

Some in luxury delighting;
More in talking than in fighting;
Lovers old, and beaux decrepit;
Lordlings empty and insipid.

Poets, painters, and musicians;
Lawyers, doctors, politicians:
Pamphlets, newspaper, and odes,
Seeking fame by different roads.

Gallant souls with empty purses,
Generals only fit for nurses;
School-boys, smit with martial spirit,
Taking place of veteran merit.

Honest men can't get places,
Knaves who show unblushing faces;
Ruin hastened, peace retarded;
Candour spurned, and art rewarded.

Mary Robinson (1795)

The Sick Rose

O ROSE, thou art sick!
   The invisible worm,
That flies in the night,
In the howling storm,

Has found out thy bed
Of crimson joy;
And his dark secret love
Does thy life destroy.

William Blake (1757–1827)

Jerusalem

AND did those feet in ancient time
   Walk upon England's mountains green?
And was the holy Lamb of God
   On England's pleasant pastures seen?

And did the Countenance Divine
   Shine forth upon our clouded hills?
And was Jerusalem builded here
   Among these dark Satanic Mills?

Bring me my bow of burning gold!
   Bring me my arrows of desire!
Bring me my spear! O clouds, unfold!
   Bring me my chariot of fire!

I will not cease from mental fight,
   Nor shall my sword sleep in my hand,
Till we have built Jerusalem
   In England's green and pleasant land.

William Blake

The Tyger

Tyger! Tyger! burning bright
In the forests of the night,
What immortal hand or eye
Could frame thy fearful symmetry?

In what distant deeps or skies
Burnt the fire of thine eyes?
On what wings dare he aspire?
What the hand dare seize the fire?

What the shoulder, and what art,
Could twist the sinews of thy heart?
And when thy heart began to beat,
What dread hand? And what dread feet?

What the hammer? What the chain?
In what furnace was thy brain?
What the anvil? What dread grasp
Dare its deadly terrors clasp?

When the stars threw down their spears,
And water'd heaven with their tears,
Did He smile His work to see?
Did He who made the Lamb make thee?

Tyger! Tyger! burning bright
In the forests of the night,
What immortal hand or eye,
Dare frame thy fearful symmetry?

William Blake

The Daffodils

I WANDER'D lonely as a cloud
   That floats on high o'er vale and hills,
When all at once I saw a crowd,
A host, of golden daffodils;
Beside the lake, beneath the trees,
Fluttering and dancing in the breeze.

Continuous as the stars that shine
And twinkle on the Milky Way,
They stretch'd in never-ending line
Along the margin of a bay:
Ten thousand saw I at a glance
Tossing their heads in sprightly dance.

The waves beside them danced, but they
Out-did the sparkling waves in glee:
A poet could not but be gay
In such a jocund company:
I gazed – and gazed – but little thought
What wealth the show to me had brought:

For oft, when on my couch I lie
In vacant or in pensive mood,
They flash upon that inward eye
Which is the bliss of solitude;
And then my heart with pleasure fills,
And dances with the daffodils.

William Wordsworth (1770–1850)

Lucy

She dwelt among the untrodden ways
   Beside the springs of Dove,
A Maid whom there were none to praise
   And very few to love:

A violet by a mossy stone
   Half hidden from the eye!
– Fair as a star, when only one
   Is shining in the sky.

She lived unknown, and few could know
   When Lucy ceased to be;
But she is in her grave, and, oh,
   The difference to me!

William Wordsworth

She Walks in Beauty

She walks in beauty, like the night
   Of cloudless climes and starry skies;
And all that's best of dark and bright
   Meet in her aspect and her eyes:
Thus mellow'd to that tender light
   Which heaven to gaudy day denies.

One shade the more, one ray the less,
   Had half impair'd the nameless grace
Which waves in every raven tress,
   Or softly lightens o'er her face;
Where thoughts serenely sweet express
   How pure, how dear their dwelling-place.

And on that cheek, and o'er that brow,
   So soft, so calm, yet eloquent,
The smiles that win, the tints that glow,
   But tell of days in goodness spent,
A mind at peace with all below,
   A heart whose love is innocent!

George, Lord Byron (1788–1824)

To Autumn

Season of mists and mellow fruitfulness,
  Close bosom-friend of the maturing sun;
Conspiring with him how to load and bless
  With fruit the vines that round the thatch-eaves run;
To bend with apples the moss'd cottage-trees,
  And fill all fruit with ripeness to the core;
    To swell the gourd, and plump the hazel shells
  With a sweet kernel; to set budding more,
And still more, later flowers for the bees,
Until they think warm days will never cease,
  For summer has o'erbrimm'd their clammy cells.

Who hath not seen thee oft amid thy store?
  Sometimes whoever seeks abroad may find
Thee sitting careless on a granary floor,
  Thy hair soft-lifted by the winnowing wind;
Or on a half-reap'd furrow sound asleep,
  Drowsed with the fume of poppies, while thy hook
    Spares the next swath and all its twined flowers:
  And sometimes like a gleaner thou dost keep
Steady thy laden head across a brook;
Or by a cider-press, with patient look,
  Thou watchest the last oozings hours by hours.

Where are the songs of Spring? Aye, where are they?
  Think not of them, thou hast thy music too,–
While barred clouds bloom the soft-dying day,
  And touch the stubble-plains with rosy hue;
Then in a wailful choir the small gnats mourn
  Among the river-shallows, borne aloft
    Or sinking as the light wind lives or dies;
  And full-grown lambs loud bleat from hilly bourn;
Hedge-crickets sing; and now with treble soft
The redbreast whistles from a garden-croft;
  And gathering swallows twitter in the skies.

John Keats (1795–1821)

'I remember, I remember'

I REMEMBER, I remember
The house where I was born,
The little window where the sun
Came peeping in at morn;
He never came a wink too soon
Nor brought too long a day;
But now, I often wish the night
Had borne my breath away.

I remember, I remember
The roses, red and white,
The violets, and the lily-cups –
Those flowers made of light!
The lilacs where the robin built,
And where my brother set
The laburnum on his birthday, –
The tree is living yet!

I remember, I remember
Where I was used to swing,
And thought the air must rush as fresh
To swallows on the wing;
My spirit flew in feathers then
That is so heavy now,
And summer pools could hardly cool
The fever on my brow.

I remember, I remember
The fir trees dark and high;
I used to think their slender tops
Were close against the sky:
It was a childish ignorance,
But now 'tis little joy
To know I'm farther off from Heaven
Than when I was a boy.

Thomas Hood (1799–1845)

Abou Ben Adhem

Abou Ben Adhem (may his tribe increase!)
Awoke one night from a deep dream of peace,
And saw, within the moonlight in his room,
Making it rich, and like a lily in bloom,
An angel writing in a book of gold:–
Exceeding peace had made Ben Adhem bold,
And to the presence in the room he said,
'What writest thou?'– The vision raised its head,
And with a look made of all sweet accord,
Answered, 'The names of those who love the Lord.'
'And is mine one?' said Abou. 'Nay, not so,'
Replied the angel. Abou spoke more low,
But cheerly still; and said, 'I pray thee then,
Write me as one that loves his fellow-men.'

The angel wrote, and vanished. The next night
It came again with a great wakening light,
And showed the names whom love of God had blessed,
And lo! Ben Adhem's name led all the rest.

James Henry Leigh Hunt (1784–1859)

'Say not the struggle nought availeth'

Say not the struggle nought availeth,
The labour and the wounds are vain,
The enemy faints not, nor faileth,
And as things have been they remain.

If hopes were dupes, fears may be liars;
It may be, in yon smoke concealed,
Your comrades chase e'en now the fliers,
And, but for you, possess the field.

For while the tired waves, vainly breaking,
Seem here no painful inch to gain,
Far back, through creeks and inlets making,
Comes silent, flooding in, the main.

And not by eastern windows only,
When daylight comes, comes in the light;
In front, the sun climbs slow, how slowly,
But westward, look, the land is bright!

Arthur Hugh Clough (1819–1861)

Stanzas

OFTEN rebuked, yet always back returning
   To those first feelings that were born with me,
And leaving busy chase of wealth and learning
   For idle dreams of things which cannot be:

To-day, I will seek not the shadowy region;
   Its unsustaining vastness waxes drear;
And visions rising, legion after legion,
   Bring the unreal world too strangely near.

I'll walk, but not in old heroic traces,
   And not in paths of high morality,
And not among the half-distinguished faces,
   The clouded forms of long-past history.

I'll walk where my own nature would be leading:
   It vexes me to choose another guide:
Where the grey flocks in ferny glens are feeding;
   Where the wild wind blows on the mountain-side.

What have those lonely mountains worth revealing?
   More glory and more grief than I can tell:
The earth that wakes *one* human heart to feeling
   Can centre both the worlds of Heaven and Hell.

Emily Brontë (1818–1848)

Dover Beach

The sea is calm to-night.
The tide is full, the moon lies fair
Upon the Straits – on the French coast, the light
Gleams, and is gone; the cliffs of England stand,
Glimmering and vast, out in the tranquil bay.

Come to the window, sweet is the night air!
Only, from the long line of spray
Where the sea meets the moon-blanched sand,
Listen! you hear the grating roar
Of pebbles which the waves suck back, and fling,
At their return, up the high strand,
Begin, and cease, and then again begin,
With tremulous cadence slow, and bring
The eternal note of sadness in.

Sophocles long ago
Heard it on the Ægæan, and it brought
Into his mind the turbid ebb and flow,
Of human misery; we
Find also in the sound a thought,
Hearing it by this distant northern sea.

The sea of faith
Was once, too, at the full, and round earth's shore
Lay like the folds of a bright girdle furled;
But now I only hear
Its melancholy, long, withdrawing roar,
Retreating to the breath
Of the night-wind down the vast edges drear
And naked shingles of the world.

Ah, love, let us be true
To one another! for the world, which seems
To lie before us like a land of dreams,
So various, so beautiful, so new,
Hath really neither joy, nor love, nor light,
Nor certitude, nor peace, nor help for pain;
And we are here as on a darkling plain
Swept with confused alarms of struggle and flight,
Where ignorant armies clash by night.

Matthew Arnold (1822–1888)

Lyrics, Odes and Elegies

'I'll tell you how the Sun rose'

I'll tell you how the Sun rose –
A Ribbon at a time –
The Steeples swam in Amethyst –
The news, like Squirrels, ran –
The Hills untied their Bonnets –
The Bobolinks* – begun –
Then I said softly to myself –
'That must have been the Sun'!
But how he set – I know not –
There seemed a purple stile
That little Yellow boys and girls
Were climbing all the while –
Till when they reached the other side,
A Dominie* in Gray –
Put gently up the evening Bars –
And led the flock away –

Emily Dickinson (1830–1886)

'I fear a Man of frugal Speech'

I fear a Man of frugal Speech –
I fear a Silent Man –
Haranguer – I can overtake –
Or Babbler – entertain –

But He who weigheth – While the Rest –
Expend their furthest pound –
Of this Man – I am wary –
I fear that He is Grand –

Emily Dickinson

* Bobolink – a North American singing bird   * Dominie – schoolmaster

'A narrow Fellow in the Grass'

A NARROW Fellow in the Grass
Occasionally rides –
You may have met Him – did you not
His notice sudden is –
The Grass divides as with a Comb –
A spotted shaft is seen –
And then it closes at your feet
And opens further on –

He likes a Boggy Acre
A Floor too cool for Corn –
Yet when a Boy, and Barefoot –
I more than once at Noon
Have passed, I thought, a Whip lash
Unbraiding in the Sun
When stooping to secure it
It wrinkled, and was gone –

Several of Nature's People
I know, and they know me –
I feel for them a transport
Of cordiality –

But never met this Fellow
Attended, or alone
Without a tighter breathing
And Zero at the Bone –

Emily Dickinson

Pied Beauty

Glory be to God for dappled things –
  For skies of couple-colour as a brinded cow;
    For rose-moles all in stipple upon trout that swim;
Fresh-firecoal chestnut-falls; finches' wings;
  Landscape plotted and pieced – fold, fallow, and plough;
    And áll trádes, their gear and tackle and trim.

All things counter, original, spare, strange;
  Whatever is fickle, freckled (who knows how?)
    With swift, slow; sweet, sour; adazzle, dim;
He fathers-forth whose beauty is past change:
                    Praise him.

Gerard Manley Hopkins (1844–1889)

Sea Love

Tide be runnin' the great world over:
  'Twas only last June month I mind that we
Was thinkin' the toss and the call in the breast of the lover
  So everlastin' as the sea.

Heer's the same little fishes that sputter and swim,
  Wi' the moon's old glim on the grey, wet sand;
An' him no more to me nor me to him
  Than the wind goin' over my hand.

Charlotte Mew (1870–1928)

Lyrics, Odes and Elegies

The Way Through the Woods

They shut the road through the woods
 Seventy years ago.
Weather and rain have undone it again,
And now you would never know
There was once a road through the woods
Before they planted the trees.
It is underneath the coppice and heath,
And the thin anemones.
Only the keeper sees
That, where the ring-dove broods,
And the badgers roll at ease,
There was once a road through the woods.

Yet, if you enter the woods
Of a summer evening late,
When the night-air cools on the trout-ringed pools
Where the otter whistles his mate,
(They fear not men in the woods,
Because they see so few)
You will hear the beat of a horse's feet,
And the swish of a skirt in the dew,
Steadily cantering through
The misty solitudes,
As though they perfectly knew
The old lost road through the woods. . . .
But there is no road through the woods.

Rudyard Kipling (1865–1936)

(opposite) 'The Graham Children', William Hogarth, 1742

Poems Published
For Children

'One old Oxford ox opening oysters'

One old Oxford ox opening oysters;
Two tee-totums totally tired of trying to trot
 to Tadbury;
Three tall tigers tippling tenpenny nails;
Four fat friars fanning fainting flies;
Five frippy Frenchmen foolishly fishing for
 flies;
Six sportsmen shooting snipes;
Seven Severn salmon swallowing shrimps;
Eight Englishmen eagerly examining Europe;
Nine nimble noblemen nibbling nonpareils;
Ten tinkers tinkling upon ten tin tinder-boxes
 with tenpenny tacks;
Eleven elephants elegantly upright;
Twelve topographical typographers typically
 translating types.

Unknown

The Birched Schoolboy

On Monday in the morning when I shall rise
At vi. of the clock, it is the gise
To go to school without a-vise
I had rather go twenty mile twice!
   What availeth it me though I say nay?

My master looketh as he were mad:
'Where hast thou been, thou sorry lad?'
'Milking ducks, my mother bade:'
It was no marvel that I were sad.
   What availeth it me though I say nay?

My master peppered my arse with well good speed:
It was worse than fennel seed;
He would not leave till it did bleed.
Much sorrow has been for his deed!
   What availeth it me though I say nay?

I would my master were a wat*
And my book a wild cat,
And a brace of greyhounds in his top.
I would be glad for to see that!
   What availeth it me though I say nay?

I would my master where an hare,
And all his bookis houndis were,
And I myself a jolly hunter:
To blow my horn I would not spare!
For if he were dead I would not care.
   What availeth it me though I say nay?

Unknown (c. 1490)

* wat – hare

The Boy Serving at Table

My dear child, first thyself enable
With all thine heart to virtuous discipline;
Afore thy sovereign, standing at the table,
Dispose thou thee after my doctrine
To all nurture thy courage to incline.
First, when thou speakest be not reckless,
Keep feet and fingers still in peace.
Be simple of cheer, cast not thine eye aside,
Gaze not about, turning thy sight over all.
Against the post let not thy back abide,
Neither make thy mirror of the wall.
Pick not thy nose, and, most especial,
Be well ware, and set hereon thy thought,
Before thy sovereign scratch nor rub thee nought.

John Lydgate (?1370–1450)

Worth Remembering

Whatsoe'er you find to do,
  Do it, boys, with all your might;
Never be "a *little* true,"
  Or "a *little* in the right."
    Trifles even
    Lead to heaven;
Trifles make the life of man;
    So in all things,
    Great or small things,
Be as THOROUGH as you can.

Let no speck their surface dim,
  Spotless truth and honour bright;
I'd not give a fig for him
  Who says that *any* lie is white!
    He who falters,
    Twists or alters
Little atoms when we speak,
    May deceive *me*,
    But believe me,
To *himself* he is a sneak!

Unknown (Appeared in Boy's Own Paper, *1884)*

The Most Lamentable and Deplorable History of the Two Children in the Wood

SHRUBLAND HALL
Deep seated in a flowery vale,
Beside a woody dell,
Stood Shrubland Hall, where, says the tale,
A worthy pair did dwell.

THE CHILDREN WITH THEIR PARENTS
Two beauteous babes this happy pair,
To crown their loves had got:
The proudest monarch on his throne,
Might envy them their lot.

THE UNCLE TAKING THE CHILDREN
But death, in midst of all their joys,
Did seize this loving pair,
Who, dying, left their girl and boy
Unto an Uncle's care.

THE UNCLE BRIBING THE RUFFIANS
But to their fortunes he aspired,
And to secure his prey,
He two unfeeling Ruffians hired
To take their lives away.

Poems Published for Children

THE RUFFIANS WITH THE CHILDREN
These wretches, cruel, fierce and bold,
Conveyed them to a wood,
There, for the sake of filthy gold,
To shed their infant blood.

THE RUFFIANS FIGHTING
But one his purpose did repent,
Before the deed was done,
And slew the other Ruffian there,
Then left the babes alone.

THE CHILDREN IN THE WOOD
Their little hearts with terror sank,
With hunger, too, they cried,
At length upon a flowery bank
They laid them down, and died.

THE CHILDREN'S DEATH.
The Redbreasts, in their clustering bowers,
Sung mournful on each spray,
And there with leaves and fragrant flowers,
O'erspread them as they lay.

18th century folk ballad (This version 1825)

C c

Captain Crackskull crack'd a Catchpoll's Cockscomb:
Did Captain Crackskull crack a Catchpoll's Cockscomb?
If Captain Crackskull crack'd a Catchpoll's Cockscomb,
Where's the Catchpoll's Cockscomb Captain Crackskull crack'd?

N n

Neddy Noodle nipp'd his Neighbour's Nutmegs:
Did Neddy Noodle nip his Neighbour's Nutmegs?
If Neddy Noodle nipp'd his Neighbour's Nutmegs,
Where are the Neighbour's Nutmegs Neddy Noodle nipp'd?

Catchpoll – sheriff's bailiff

Cockscomb – fool's cap or ludicrous term for head

O o

Oliver Oglethorpe ogled an Owl and Oyster:
Did Oliver Oglethorpe ogle an Owl and Oyster?
If Oliver Oglethorpe ogled an Owl and Oyster,
Where are the Owl and Oyster Oliver Oglethorpe ogled?

P p

Peter Piper pick'd a Peck of Pepper:
Did Peter Piper pick a Peck of Pepper?
If Peter Piper pick'd a Peck of Pepper,
Where's the Peck of Pepper Peter Piper pick'd?

Unknown (From Peter Piper's Practical Principles of Plain and Perfect Pronunciation, *1813)*

Little Jack Jingle

Little Jack Jingle,
Played truant at school,
They made his bum tingle
For being a fool;
He promised no more
Like a fool he would look
But be a good boy and attend to his book.

Little Jack Jingle,
    Went to court Suky Shingle,
Says he, shall we mingle
    Our toes in the bed;
Fye! Jacky Jingle,
    Says little Suky Shingle,
We must try to mingle,
    Our pence for some bread.

Suky you shall be my wife,
    And I'll tell you why;
I have got a little pig,
    And you have got a sty;
I have got a dun cow,
    And you can make good cheese,
Suky will you have me?
    Say yes, if you please.

Unknown (c. 1800)

A Visit to the Lunatic Asylum

Come child with me, a father said,
I often have a visit paid
To yon receptacle of woe,
For Lunatics. – Come, child, and know,
And prize the blessing you possess,
And prove the feeling you profess.
Come, shed a tear o'er those devoid
Of what you have through life enjoy'd:
See, in this mansion of distress,
The throngs of those who don't possess
Their reason; but with constant moan
Cast ashes on her vacant throne;
Her sceptre cankering in the dust,
Fair reason weeping o'er the rust;
Her seat deserted, fallen, decay,
And midnight horrors shade fair day.
Reason, thy grateful cheering light
Entomb'd 'neath ashes, clad in night,
Lays prostrate – where thy being's ceas'd,
Thy sons are levell'd with the beast.

   What means that horrid dreadful yell,
Those screeches from yon grated cell;
The frightful clinking of the chain,
And wild effusions of the brain?

   How madly now he tears his hair,
What wildness mixes with his stare;
With rage he rends his tatter'd clothes,
More vicious and still stronger grows.
What awful wreathings vent in rage,
With eye-balls starting, dread presage;
My God! can creature man thus sink,
Plung'd headlong down th' appalling brink.

   Point out the man who grateful shows
That he the worth of reason knows;
That he his reason holds from God,
And stays by gratitude the rod
That might afflict – that might chastise –
The man who does the gift despise.

   Were reason's channels choak'd and dried,
You of her benefits denied;
Read here what you would surely be,
Your picture in these inmates see.

   Who could withhold a grateful heart,
For the possession of that part
Which lifts the mortal from the beast?
Yes, gratitude it claims at least.

   But, oh! possessor ever know,
If gratitude you'd truly show,
Let every reasoning power be given
Up to the service of kind Heav'n.

Henry Sharpe Horsley (1828)

Sad Effects of Gunpowder

"I have got a sad story to tell,"
   Said Betty one day to Mamma:
"T'will be long, Ma'am, before John is well,
On his eye is so dreadful a scar.

"Master Wilful enticed him away,
   To join with some more little boys;
They went in the garden to play,
   And I soon heard a terrible noise.

"Master Wilful had laid a long train
   Of Gunpowder, Ma'am, on the wall;
It has put them to infinite pain,
   For it blew up, and injured them all.

"John's eyebrow is totally bare;
   Tom's nose is bent out of its place;
Sam Bushy has lost all his hair,
   And Dick White is quite black in the face."

Unknown (1831)

The Results of Stealing a Pin

A LAD when at school, one day stole a pin,
And said that no harm was in such a small sin,
He next stole a knife, and said 'twas a trifle;
Next thing he did was pockets to rifle,
Next thing he did was a house to break in,
The next thing – upon a gallows to swing.
So let us avoid all little sinnings,
Since such is the end of petty beginnings.

Unknown (1821)

Give with Prudence

"I SEE, Mamma," said little Jane,
"A beggar coming down the lane;
O, let me take him (may not I?)
This cheesecake and some currant pie."

"Your charity I much approve,
And something you may take him, love;
But let it be some bread and cheese,
Much better than such things as these.

"By giving sweetmeats to the poor,
Who never tasted them before,
We spoil the good we have in view,
And teach them wants they never knew."

Unknown (1834)

The Umbrella

Once as little Isabella
Ventured, with a large Umbrella,
Out upon a rainy day,
She was nearly blown away.

Luckily her good Mamma
Saw her trouble from afar;
Running just in time, she caught her
Pretty little flying daughter.

Unknown (1834)

Thoughtless Julia

Julia did in the window stand;
  Mamma, then sitting by,
Saw her put out her little hand
  And try to catch a fly.

"O do not hurt the pretty thing,"
  Her prudent Mother said;
"Crush not its leg or feeble wing,
  So beautifully made.

"In Papa's book, 'Take not away
  The life you cannot give,
For all things have' (you'll read one day)
  'An equal right to live.'"

Unknown (1834)

The Dreadful Story about Harriet and the Matches

It almost makes me cry to tell
What foolish Harriet befell.
Mamma and Nurse went out one day
And left her all alone at play;
Now, on the table close at hand,
A box of matches chanc'd to stand;
And kind Mamma and Nurse had told her,
That, if she touch'd them, they should scold her.
But Harriet said: "O, what a pity!
For, when they burn, it is so pretty;
They crackle so, and spit, and flame;
Mamma, too, often does the same."

The pussy-cats heard this,
And they began to hiss,
And stretch their claws
And raise their paws;
"Me-ow," they said, "me-ow, me-o,
You'll burn to death, if you do so."

But Harriet would not take advice,
She lit a match, it was so nice!
It crackled so, it burn'd so clear, –
Exactly like the picture here.
She jump'd for joy and ran about
And was too pleas'd to put it out.

The pussy-cats saw this
And said: "Oh, naughty, naughty Miss!"
And stretch'd their claws
And rais'd their paws:
"'Tis very, very wrong, you know,
Me-ow, me-o, me-ow, me-o,
You will be burnt, if you do so".

And see! Oh! what a dreadful thing!
The fire has caught her apron-string;
Her apron burns, her arms, her hair;
She burns all over, everywhere.

Then how the pussy-cats did mew,
What else, poor pussies, could they do?
They scream'd for help, 'twas all in vain!
So then, they said: "we'll scream again;
Make haste, make haste, me-ow, me-o,
She'll burn to death, we told her so."

So she was burnt, with all her clothes,
And arms, and hands, and eyes, and nose;
Till she had nothing more to lose
Except her little scarlet shoes;
And nothing else but these was found
Among her ashes on the ground.

And when the good cats sat beside
The smoking ashes, how they cried!
"Me-ow, me-oo, me-ow, me-oo,
What will Mamma and Nursy do?"
Their tears ran down their cheeks so fast;
They made a little pond at last.

Heinrich Hoffman 1844
(Translated from the German)

Dear Mother, Let me Go!

'Mother, dear mother, do not seek
To keep me from my Saviour's breast;
Oh, dry those sad tears from thy cheek,
Thy darling soon will be at rest.

Oh, would you keep me, mother dear,
From Him who ever loved me so?
I do not wish to linger here;
Mother, dear mother, let me go!

I seem to hear my Saviour's voice,
I seem to see His gentle smile;
Oh, mother, can you not rejoice?
We'll part but for a little while.

'For sinners such as she I died,'
I seem to hear Him say to thee;
'Keep not my ransomed from my side,
But let thy darling come to Me.'

With praise to Him who died for me,
Mother your heart should overflow;
Then do not seek to hinder me,
Mother, dear mother, let me go!'

'Yes,' cried the mother, 'Go, my child;
The Saviour calls – He loves you best;'
Mary looked up and sweetly smiled,
Then closed her eyes – and was at rest.

Unknown (*From* The Sunday School Magazine, *1853*)

'Fear No NME'

I'll sing a song of A B C
(If you will list awhile,
And pay attention unto me)
That may create a smile.
Not many children, I'll suppose,
But do their letters know;
And therefore I shall sing to them
A song of the *Cross row*.

Both U and I with EE's can C
That man is prone to ill,
And that to B or not to B,
Is the 'great question' still.
Would we preserve our character,
And not our minds abuse,
We must be careful not to R,
And mind our P's and Q's.

A man cannot get on in life,
Unless that he is Y Y's;
And to avoid all snares and strife,
Must make use of his I I's.
In bus'ness would he make his way,
And take care not to lose,
He must look sharp to L S D,*
And shun the I O U's.

In all that you are called to do,
Endeavour to X L;
For X L N C is a thing
That rarely fails to tell.
Who puzzles much Z is wrong,
Yet be not over dull,
For it must be a wretched thing
To have an M T skull.

B B C as a B C B,
In village or C T;
In quiet temper ever walk,
And life will E C B.
For those that R still feel P T,
And follow on S T;
Do what is right, walk in the light,
And fear no N M E.

Be careful that you shun X S
When you to make S A,
In meal or drink, or every mess
May hasten your D K.
And dying you will leave behind,
Instead of L E G,
To turn the nose and taint the wind,
A rank X U V E.

Make principle your A and Z,
And pattern F E G;
And then your course of duty will
Be right unto a T.
And when that you shall C C's to B
A living N T T,
In this sad world, in that above,
U L live in X T C.

William Martin (From
The Birthday Gift, 1861)

* LSD: pre-decimal, standing for Pounds, Shillings and Pence

The Blind Men and the Elephant

It was six men of Indostan
   To learning much inclined,
Who went to see the Elephant
   (Though all of them were blind),
That each by observation
   Might satisfy his mind.

The *First* approached the Elephant,
   And happening to fall
Against his broad and sturdy side,
   At once began to bawl:
"God bless me! but the Elephant
   Is very like a wall!"

The *Second*, feeling of the tusk,
   Cried, "Ho! what have we here
So very round and smooth and sharp?
   To me 'tis mighty clear
This wonder of an Elephant
   Is very like a spear!"

The *Third* approached the animal,
   And happening to take
The squirming trunk within his hands,
   Thus boldly up and spake:
"I see," quoth he, "the Elephant
   Is very like a snake!"

The *Fourth* reached out an eager hand,
   And felt about the knee.
"What most this wondrous beast is like
   Is mighty plain," quoth he;
"'Tis clear enough the Elephant
   Is very like a tree!"

The *Fifth* who chanced to touch the ear,
   Said: "E'en the blindest man
Can tell what this resembles most;
   Deny the fact who can,
This marvel of an Elephant
   Is very like a fan!"

The *Sixth* no sooner had begun
   About the beast to grope,
Than, seizing on the swinging tail
   That fell within his scope,
"I see," quoth he, "the Elephant
   Is very like a rope!"

And so these men of Indostan
   Disputed loud and long,
Each in his own opinion
   Exceeding stiff and strong,
Though each was partly in the right,
   And all were in the wrong!

   Moral
So oft in theologic wars,
   The disputants, I ween,
Rail on in utter ignorance
   Of what each other mean,
And prate about an Elephant
   Not one of them has seen!

John Godfrey Saxe (1816 – 1887)

Jabberwocky

'Twas brillig, and the slithy toves
  Did gyre and gimble in the wabe:
All mimsy were the borogoves,
  And the mome raths outgrabe.

'Beware the Jabberwock, my son!
  The jaws that bite, the claws that catch!
Beware the Jubjub bird, and shun
  The frumious Bandersnatch!'

He took his vorpal sword in hand:
  Long time the manxome foe he sought –
So rested he by the Tumtum tree,
  And stood awhile in thought.

And, as in uffish thought he stood,
  The Jabberwock, with eyes of flame,
Came whiffling through the tulgey wood,
  And burbled as it came!

One, two! One, two! And through and through
  The vorpal blade went snicker-snack!
He left it dead, and with its head
  He went galumphing back.

'And hast thou slain the Jabberwock!
  Come to my arms, my beamish boy!
O frabjous day! Callooh! Callay!'
  He chortled in his joy.

'Twas brillig, and the slithy toves
  Did gyre and gimble in the wabe;
All mimsy were the borogoves,
  And the mome raths outgrabe.

Lewis Carroll (*From* Through the Looking Glass, *1872*)

The Lobster Quadrille

'Will you walk a little faster?' said a whiting to a snail.
   'There's a porpoise close behind us, and he's treading on my tail.
See how eagerly the lobsters and the turtles all advance!
They are waiting on the shingle – will you come and join the dance?
   Will you, won't you, will you, won't you, will you join the dance?
   Will you, won't you, will you, won't you, won't you join the dance?

'You can really have no notion how delightful it will be,
When they take us up and throw us, with the lobsters, out to sea!'
But the snail replied 'Too far, too far!' and gave a look askance –
Said he thanked the whiting kindly, but he would not join the dance.
   Would not, could not, would not, could not, would not join the dance.
   Would not, could not, would not, could not, could not join the dance.

'What matters it how far we go?' his scaly friend replied.
'There is another shore, you know, upon the other side.
The further off from England the nearer is to France –
Then turn not pale, beloved snail, but come and join the dance.
   Will you, won't you, will you, won't you, will you join the dance?
   Will you, won't you, will you, won't you, won't you join the dance?"

Lewis Carroll (From Alice's Adventures in Wonderland, *1865)*

The Courtship of the Yonghy-Bonghy-Bò

On the Coast of Coromandel
  Where the early pumpkins blow,
In the middle of the woods
  Lived the Yonghy-Bonghy-Bò.
Two old chairs, and half a candle, –
One old jug without a handle, –
    These were all his worldly goods:
    In the middle of the woods,
    These were all the worldly goods,
Of the Yonghy-Bonghy-Bò,
Of the Yonghy-Bonghy-Bò.

Once, among the Bong-trees walking
  Where the early pumpkins blow,
    To a little heap of stones
  Came the Yonghy-Bonghy-Bò.
There he heard a Lady talking,
To some milk-white Hens of Dorking, –
    ''Tis the Lady Jingly Jones!
    'On that little heap of stones
    'Sits the Lady Jingly Jones!'
Said the Yonghy-Bonghy-Bò,
Said the Yonghy-Bonghy-Bò.

'Lady Jingly! Lady Jingly!
  'Sitting where the pumpkins blow,
    'Will you come and be my wife?'
  Said the Yonghy-Bonghy-Bò.
'I am tired of living singly, –
'On this coast so wild and shingly, –
    'I'm a-weary of my life:
    'If you'll come and be my wife,
    'Quite serene would be my life' –
Said the Yonghy-Bonghy-Bò,
Said the Yonghy-Bonghy-Bò.

'On this Coast of Coromandel,
  'Shrimps and watercresses grow,
    'Prawns are plentiful and cheap,'
  Said the Yonghy-Bonghy-Bò.
'You shall have my Chairs and candle,
'And my jug without a handle! –
    'Gaze upon the rolling deep
    ('Fish is plentiful and cheap)
    'As the sea, my love is deep!'
Said the Yonghy-Bonghy-Bò,
Said the Yonghy-Bonghy-Bò.

Lady Jingly answered sadly,
   And her tears began to flow, –
     'Your proposal comes too late,
   'Mr. Yonghy-Bonghy-Bò!
'I would be your wife most gladly!'
(Here she twirled her fingers madly,)
     'But in England I've a mate!
   'Yes! you've asked me far too late,
   'For in England I've a mate,
'Mr. Yonghy-Bonghy-Bò!
'Mr. Yonghy-Bonghy-Bò!'

'Mr. Jones – (his name is Handel, –
   'Handel Jones, Esquire, & Co.)
     'Dorking fowls delights to send,
   'Mr. Yonghy-Bonghy-Bò!
'Keep, oh! keep your chairs and candle,
'And your jug without a handle, –
     'I can merely be your friend!
   '– Should my Jones more Dorkings send,
   'I will give you three, my friend!
'Mr. Yonghy-Bonghy-Bò!
'Mr. Yonghy-Bonghy-Bò!'

'Though you've such a tiny body,
   'And your head so large doth grow, –
     'Though your hat may blow away,
   'Mr. Yonghy-Bonghy-Bò!
'Though you're such a Hoddy Doddy –
'Yet I wish that I could modi-
     'fy the words I needs must say!
   'Will you please to go away?
   'That is all I have to say –
'Mr. Yonghy-Bonghy-Bò!
'Mr. Yonghy-Bonghy-Bò!'

Down the slippery slopes of Myrtle,
   Where the early pumpkins blow,
     To the calm and silent sea
   Fled the Yonghy-Bonghy-Bò.
There, beyond the Bay of Gurtle,
Lay a large and lively Turtle; –
     'You're the Cove,' he said, 'for me
   'On your back beyond the sea,
   'Turtle, you shall carry me!'
Said the Yonghy-Bonghy-Bò,
Said the Yonghy-Bonghy-Bò.

Through the silent-roaring ocean
  Did the Turtle swiftly go;
    Holding fast upon his shell
  Rode the Yonghy-Bonghy-Bò.
With a sad primæval motion
Towards the sunset isles of Boshen
  Still the Turtle bore him well.
  Holding fast upon his shell,
  'Lady Jingly Jones, farewell!'
Sang the Yonghy-Bonghy-Bò,
Sang the Yonghy-Bonghy-Bò.

From the Coast of Coromandel,
  Did that Lady never go;
    On that heap of stones she mourns
  For the Yonghy-Bonghy-Bò.
On that Coast of Coromandel,
In his jug without a handle
  Still she weeps, and daily moans;
  On that little heap of stones
  To her Dorking Hens she moans,
For the Yonghy-Bonghy-Bò,
For the Yonghy-Bonghy-Bò.

Edward Lear (1812–1888)

Muff Brown

Week in, week out, straight through the terms,
    At the foot of the form he sat,
With his simple face and sandy hair,
    And queer eyes like a bat.
And if ever he did get up a place
    He was safe to be taken down;
But nobody heeded him, down or up –
    He was only old "Muff Brown."

In the playing-fields it was much the same,
    We dubbed Sam Brown a flat;
Slow on the river, and slow at the goals,
    And no end of a muff with the bat.
Alone about the school-ground Sam
    Went mooning up and down,
For none of the fellows cared too much
    To chum with old Muff Brown.

Our school days over we scattered far,
    Like leaves before the breeze,
And some went east and some went west,
    And some beyond the seas.
Some climbed life's ladder rung by rung
    And won a fair renown;
Yet never a word had I ever heard
    Of how it fared with Brown.

But yesterday in a supplement
    Of the "Times" I wondering read
Of a little band through a wild lone land
    By one white captain led.
A story of peril and toil and pain,
    Of marches long and lonely;
Of a hope forlorn seven months upborne
    By the word of that white man only.

Safe to the goal he led them on,
    With a heart no fear could daunt,
And the story reads like the magic deeds
    In the tales of old romaunt.
All England rings with one name to-day,
    And the victor's shining crown
It's here as plain as the "Times" can print
    They are giving to old Muff Brown.

Robert Richardson (1884)

(opposite) 'Rejected', John Millais, 1853

Narratives

Sir Gawain and the Green Knight (extract)

The grene knight upon grounde graythly him dresses,
A littel lutte with the hed, the lyre he discoveres,
His long lovely lokkes he layd over his croun,
Let the naked nek to the note schewe.
Gawayn gripped to his axe and gederes hit on hyght.
The kay fote on the folde he before sette,
Let hit doun lyghtly light on the naked,
That the scharp of the schalk schyndered the bones
And schrank thurgh the schyre grece and schadde hit in
    twynne,
That the bit of the broun stele bote on the grounde.
The fayr hed fro the halse hitte to the erthe,
That fele hit foyned with her fete there hit forth rolled.
The blode brayde fro the body, that blykked on the grene,
And nauther faltered ne fel the freke never the helder,
Bot stythly he start forth upon stif schankes
And runischly he raght out there as renkes stoden,
Laght to his lovely hed and lyft hit up sone,
And sithen bowes to his blonk, the brydel he caches,
Steppes into stele-bawe and strydes aloft,
And his hed by the here in his hande holdes,
And as sadly the segge him in his sadel sette
As none unhap had him ayled, thagh hedles he were
      In stedde.
  He brayde his bluk aboute,
  That ugly body that bledde;
  Mony one of him had doute
  By that his resouns were redde.

Unknown (c. 1400)

THE Green Knight at once took up his stance; bending his head a little, he exposed the flesh; throwing his beautiful long locks forward over his head, he let the naked neck appear in readiness. Gawain took a grip on his axe, and, lifting it up high, with the left foot advanced, brought it down deftly on the naked flesh, so that the man's own sharp weapon cleaved his bones, and sank through the fair flesh, severing it in two, so that the bright steel blade bit into the ground. The handsome head fell from the neck to the floor, and many spurned it with their feet as it rolled towards them; the blood spurted from the body and glistened on the green garments. And yet the man neither staggered at all nor fell as a result, but undismayed he sprang forward upon firm legs, and fiercely he reached out amongst the people's feet, seized his handsome head, and quickly lifted it up; and then, turning to his horse, caught the bridle, stepped into the stirrup and vaulted up, holding his head by the hair in his hand, and the knight seated himself in his saddle as calmly as if he had suffered no mishap, though he sat there headless now. He twisted his trunk around, that gruesome bleeding corpse; many were afraid of him by the time he had had his say.

Modern English version by W.R.J. Barron

The General Prologue to the Canterbury Tales (extracts)

A group of pilgrims, including the poet Geoffrey Chaucer, gather together to ride to Canterbury. Here are four of the travellers as Chaucer describes them.

With hym ther was his sone, a yong *Squier*,
A lovyere and a lusty bacheler,
With lokkes crulle as they were leyd in presse.
Of twenty yeer of age he was, I gesse.
Of his stature he was of evene lengthe,
And wonderly delyvere, and of greet strengthe.
And he hadde been somtyme in chyvachie
In Flaundres, in Artoys, and Pycardie,
And born hym weel, as of so litel space,
In hope to stonden in his lady grace.
Embrouded was he, as it were a meede
Al ful of fresshe floures, whyte and reede.
Syngynge he was, or floytynge, al the day;
He was as fressh as is the month of May.
Short was his gowne, with sleves longe and wyde.
Wel koude he sitte on hors and faire ryde.
He koude songes make and wel endite,
Juste and eek daunce, and weel purtreye and write.
So hoote he lovede that by nyghtertale
He sleep namoore than dooth a nyghtyngale.
Curteis he was, lowely, and servysable,
And carf biforn his fader at the table.

Geoffrey Chaucer (1340–1400)

He had his son with him, a fine young *Squire*,
A lover and cadet, a lad of fire
With curly locks, as if they had been pressed.
He was some twenty years of age, I guessed.
In stature he was of a moderate length,
With wonderful agility and strength.
He'd seen some service with the cavalry
In Flanders and Artois and Picardy
And had done valiantly in little space
Of time, in hope to win his lady's grace.
He was embroidered like a meadow bright
And full of freshest flowers, red and white.
Singing he was, or fluting all the day;
He was as fresh as is the month of May.
Short was his gown, the sleeves were long and wide;
He knew the way to sit a horse and ride.
He could make songs and poems and recite,
Knew how to joust and dance, to draw and write.
He loved so hotly that till dawn grew pale
He slept as little as a nightingale.
Courteous he was, lowly and serviceable,
And carved to serve his father at the table.

Modern English version by Neville Coghill

A GOOD *wif* was ther of biside *bathe*,
But she was somdel deef, and that was scathe.
Of clooth-makyng she hadde swich an haunt,
She passed hem of Ypres and of Gaunt.
In al the parisshe wif ne was ther noon
That to the offrynge bifore hire sholde goon;
And if ther dide, certeyn so wrooth was she,
That she was out of alle charitee.
Hir coverchiefs ful fyne weren of ground;
I dorste swere they weyeden ten pound
That on a Sonday weren upon hir heed.
Hir hosen weren of fyn scarlet reed,
Ful streite yteyd, and shoes ful moyste and newe.
Boold was hir face, and fair, and reed of hewe.
She was a worthy womman al hir lyve:
Housbondes at chirche dore she hadde fyve,
Withouten oother compaignye in youthe, –
But therof nedeth nat to speke as nowthe.
And thries hadde she been at Jerusalem;
She hadde passed many a straunge strem;
At Rome she hadde been, and at Boloigne,
In Galice at Seint-Jame, and at Coloigne.
She koude muchel of wandrynge by the weye.
Gat-tothed was she, soothly for to seye.
Upon an amblere esily she sat,
Ywympled wel, and on hir heed an hat
As brood as is a bokeler or a targe;
A foot-mantel aboute hir hipes large,
And on hir feet a paire of spores sharpe.
In felaweshipe wel koude she laughe and carpe.
Of remedies of love she knew per chaunce,
For she koude of that art the olde daunce.

Geoffrey Chaucer

Narratives

A worthy *woman* from beside *Bath* city
Was with us, somewhat deaf, which was a pity.
In making cloth she showed so great a bent
She bettered those of Ypres and of Ghent.
In all the parish not a dame dared stir
Towards the altar steps in front of her,
And if indeed they did, so wrath was she
As to be quite put out of charity.
Her kerchiefs were of finely woven ground;
I dared have sworn they weighed a good ten pound,
The ones she wore on Sunday, on her head.
Her hose were of the finest scarlet red
And gartered tight; her shoes were soft and new.
Bold was her face, handsome, and red in hue.
A worthy woman all her life, what's more
She'd had five husbands, all at the church door,
Apart from other company in youth;
No need just now to speak of that, forsooth.
And she had thrice been to Jerusalem,
Seen many strange rivers and passed over them;
She'd been to Rome and also to Boulogne,
St James of Compostella and Cologne,
And she was skilled in wandering by the way.
She had gap-teeth, set widely, truth to say.
Easily on an ambling horse she sat
Well wimpled up, and on her head a hat
As broad as is a buckler or a shield;
She had a flowing mantle that concealed
Large hips, her heels spurred sharply under that.
In company she liked to laugh and chat
And knew the remedies for love's mischances,
An art in which she knew the oldest dances.

Modern English version by Neville Coghill

Narratives

THE *Millere* was a stout carl for the nones;
Ful byg he was of brawn, and eek of bones.
That proved wel, for over al ther he cam,
At wrastlynge he wolde have alwey the ram.
He was short-sholdred, brood, a thikke knarre;
Ther was no dore that he nolde heve of harre,
Or breke it at a rennyng with his heed.
His berd as any sowe or fox was reed,
And therto brood, as though it were a spade.
Upon the cop right of his nose he hade
A werte, and theron stood a toft of herys,
Reed as the brustles of a sowes erys;
His nosethirles blake were and wyde.
A swerd and bokeler bar he by his syde.
His mouth as greet was as a greet forneys.
He was a janglere and a goliardeys.
And that was moost of synne and harlotries.
Wel koude he stelen corn and tollen thries;
And yet he hadde a thombe of gold, pardee.
A whit cote and a blew hood wered he.
A baggepipe wel koude he blowe and sowne,
And therwithal he broghte us out of towne.

Geoffrey Chaucer

THE *Miller* was a chap of sixteen stone,
A great stout fellow big in brawn and bone.
He did well out of them, for he could go
And win the ram at any wrestling show.
Broad, knotty and short-shouldered, he would boast
He could heave any door off hinge and post,
Or take a run and break it with his head.
His beard, like any sow or fox, was red
And broad as well, as though it were a spade;
And, at its very tip, his nose displayed
A wart on which there stood a tuft of hair
Red as the bristles in an old sow's ear.
His nostrils were as black as they were wide,
He had a sword and buckler at his side,
His mighty mouth was like a furnace door.
A wrangler and buffoon, he had a store
Of tavern stories, filthy in the main.
His was a master-hand at stealing grain.
He felt it with his thumb and thus he knew
Its quality and took three times his due –
A thumb of gold, by God, to gauge an oat!
He wore a hood of blue and a white coat.
He liked to play his bagpipes up and down
And that was how he brought us out of town.

Modern English Version by Neville Coghill

A *Clerk* ther was of *Oxenford* also,
That unto logyk hadde longe ygo.
As leene was his hors as is a rake,
And he nas nat right fat, I undertake,
But looked holwe, and therto sobrely.
Ful thredbare was his overeste courtepy;
For he hadde geten hym yet no benefice,
Ne was so worldly for to have office.
For hym was levere have at his beddes
   heed
Twenty bookes, clad in blak or reed,
Of Aristotle and his philosophie,
Than robes riche, or fithele, or gay sautrie.
But al be that he was a philosophre,
Yet hadde he but litel gold in cofre;
But al that he myghte of his freendes
   hente,
On bookes and on lernynge he it spente,
And bisily gan for the soules preye
Of hem that yaf hym wherwith to scoleye.
Of studie took he moost cure and moost
   heede.
Noght o word spak he moore than was
   neede,
And that was seyd in forme and reverence,
And short and quyk and ful of hy sentence;
Sownynge in moral vertu was his speche,
And gladly wolde he lerne and gladly
   teche.

Geoffrey Chaucer

Narratives

There was an *Oxford Cleric* too, a student,
Long given to Logic, longer than was prudent;
The horse he had was leaner than a rake,
And he was not too fat, I undertake,
But had a hollow look, a sober stare;
The thread upon his overcoat was bare.
He had found no preferment in the church
And he was too unworldly to make search.
He thought far more of having by his bed
His twenty books all bound in black and red,
Of Aristotle and philosophy
Than of gay music, fiddles or finery.
Though a philosopher, as I have told,
He had not found the stone for making gold.
Whatever money from his friends he took
He spent on learning or another book
And prayed for them most earnestly, returning
Thanks to them thus for paying for his learning.
His only care was study, and indeed
He never spoke a word more than was need,
Formal at that, respectful in the extreme,
Short, to the point, and lofty in his theme.
The thought of moral virtue filled his speech
And he would gladly learn, and gladly teach.

Modern English Version by Neville Coghill

Kubla Khan

In Xanadu did Kubla Khan
A stately pleasure-dome decree:
Where Alph, the sacred river, ran
Through caverns measureless to man
   Down to a sunless sea.

So twice five miles of fertile ground
With walls and towers were girdled round:
And here were gardens bright with sinuous rills,
Where blossomed many an incense-bearing tree,
And here were forests ancient as the hills,
Enfolding sunny spots of greenery.

But oh! that deep romantic chasm which slanted
Down the green hill athwart a cedarn cover!
A savage place; as holy and enchanted
As e'er beneath a waning moon was haunted
By woman wailing for her demon-lover!
And from this chasm, with ceaseless turmoil seething,
As if this earth in fast thick pants were breathing,
A mighty fountain momently was forced,
Amid whose swift half-intermitted burst
Huge fragments vaulted like rebounding hail,
Or chaffy grain beneath the thresher's flail:
And 'mid these dancing rocks at once and ever
It flung up momently the sacred river.
Five miles meandering with a mazy motion
Through wood and dale the sacred river ran,
Then reached the caverns measureless to man,
And sank in tumult to a lifeless ocean:
And 'mid this tumult Kubla heard from far
Ancestral voices prophesying war!

The shadow of the dome of pleasure
Floated midway on the waves;
Where was heard the mingled measure
From the fountain and the caves.
It was a miracle of rare device,
A sunny pleasure-dome with caves of ice!

   A damsel with a dulcimer
   In a vision once I saw:
   It was an Abyssinian maid,
   And on her dulcimer she played,
   Singing of Mount Abora.
   Could I revive within me
   Her symphony and song,
To such a deep delight 'twould win me,
That with music loud and long,
I would build that dome in air,
That sunny dome! those caves of ice!
And all who heard should see them there,
And all should cry, Beware! Beware!
His flashing eyes, his floating hair!
Weave a circle round him thrice,
And close your eyes with holy dread,
For he on honey dew hath fed,
And drunk the milk of Paradise.

Samuel Taylor Coleridge (1772–1834)

Peter Grimes

Peter Grimes is the son of a virtuous fisherman, but Peter grows up violent and relishes drinking, gambling and crime. When his father dies, Peter continues to fish but with a lust for power, he takes on first one and then another workhouse boy as an apprentice. Each quickly dies as a result of his neglect and cruelty, yet, in spite of the clamour raised by other seamen and their wives, he is allowed to take on a third 'of manners soft and mild'.

    Passive he labour'd, till his slender frame
Bent with his loads, and he at length was lame; –
Strange that a frame so weak could bear so long
The grossest insult and the foulest wrong;
But there were causes – in the town they gave
Fire, food, and comfort, to the gentle slave;
And though stern Peter, with a cruel hand,
And knotted rope, enforced the rude command,
Yet he consider'd what he'd lately felt,
And his vile blows with selfish pity dealt.
   One day such draughts the cruel fisher made
He could not vend them in his borough-trade,
But sail'd for London-mart; the boy was ill,
But ever humbled to his master's will;
And on the river, where they smoothly sail'd,
He strove with terror and awhile prevail'd;
But, new to danger on the angry sea,
He clung affrighten'd to his master's knee.
The boat grew leaky and the wind was strong,
Rough was the passage and the time was long;
His liquor fail'd, and Peter's wrath arose –
No more is known – the rest we must suppose,
Or learn of Peter; – Peter says, he 'spied
'The stripling's danger and for harbour tried;
'Meantime the fish, and then th' apprentice died'.
   The pitying women raised a clamour round,
And weeping said, 'Thou hast thy 'prentice drown'd'.
   Now the stern man was summon'd to the hall,
To tell his tale before the burghers all.
He gave th' account; profess'd the lad he loved,
And kept his brazen features all unmoved.

  The mayor himself with tone severe replied, –
'Henceforth with thee shall never boy abide;
'Hire thee a freeman, whom thou durst not beat,
'But who, in thy despite, will sleep and eat.
'Free thou art now! – again shouldst thou appear,
'Thou'lt find thy sentence, like thy soul, severe.'
  Alas! for Peter not a helping hand,
So was he hated, could he now command;
Alone he row'd his boat; alone he cast
His nets beside, or made his anchor fast;
To hold a rope or hear a curse was none –
He toil'd and rail'd; he groan'd and swore alone.
  Thus by himself compell'd to live each day,
To wait for certain hours the tide's delay;
At the same times the same dull views to see,
The bounding marsh-bank and the blighted tree;
The water only when the tides were high;
When low, the mud half-cover'd and half-dry;
The sun-burnt tar that blisters on the planks,
And bank-side stakes in their uneven ranks;
Heaps of entangled weeds that slowly float,
As the tide rolls by the impeded boat.
  When tides were neap, and, in the sultry day,
Through the tall bounding mud-banks made their way,
Which on each side rose swelling, and below
The dark warm flood ran silently and slow:
There anchoring, Peter chose from man to hide,
There hang his head, and view the lazy tide
In its hot slimy channel slowly glide;
Where the small eels that left the deeper way
For the warm shore, within the shallows play;
Where gaping mussels, left upon the mud,
Slope their slow passage to the fallen flood: –
Here dull and hopeless he'd lie down and trace
How sidelong crabs had scrawl'd their crooked race;
Or sadly listen to the tuneless cry
Of fishing gull or clanging golden-eye;
What time the sea-birds to the marsh would come,
And the loud bittern, from the bull-rush home,
Gave from the salt-ditch side the bellowing boom.
He nursed the feelings these dull scenes produce,
And loved to stop beside the opening sluice;
Where the small stream, confined in narrow bound,

Ran with a dull, unvaried, sadd'ning sound;
Where all presented to the eye or ear
Oppress'd the soul with misery, grief, and fear.
   Besides these objects, there were places three,
Which Peter seem'd with certain dread to see;
When he drew near them he would turn from each,
And loudly whistle till he pass'd the reach.
   A change of scene to him brought no relief;
In town, 'twas plain, men took him for a thief:
The sailors' wives would stop him in the street,
And say, 'Now, Peter, thou'st no boy to beat';
   Infants at play, when they perceived him, ran,
Warning each other – 'That's the wicked man';
He growl'd an oath, and in an angry tone
Cursed the whole place and wish'd to be alone.
   Alone he was, the same dull scenes in view,
And still more gloomy in his sight they grew.
Though man he hated, yet employ'd alone
At bootless labour, he would swear and groan,
Cursing the shoals that glided by the spot,
And gulls that caught them when his arts could not.
Cold nervous tremblings shook his sturdy frame,
And strange disease – he couldn't say the name;
Wild were his dreams, and oft he rose in fright,
Waked by his view of horrors in the night –
Horrors that would the sternest minds amaze,
Horrors that demons might be proud to raise;
And, though he felt forsaken, grieved at heart,
To think he lived from all mankind apart;
Yet, if a man approach'd, in terrors he would start.

George Crabbe (1754–1832)

La Belle Dame Sans Merci

O what can ail thee, knight-at-arms,
   Alone and palely loitering?
The sedge is wither'd from the lake,
   And no birds sing.

O what can ail thee, knight-at arms,
   So haggard and so woe-begone?
The squirrel's granary is full,
   And the harvest's done.

I see a lily on thy brow,
   With anguish moist and fever dew;
And on thy cheek a fading rose
   Fast withereth too.

I met a lady in the meads
   Full beautiful, a faery's child;
Her hair was long, her foot was light,
   And her eyes were wild –

I made a garland for her head,
   And bracelets too, and fragrant zone;
She look'd at me as she did love,
   And made sweet moan –

I set her on my pacing steed,
   And nothing else saw all day long;
For sideways would she lean, and sing
   A faery's song –

She found me roots of relish sweet,
   And honey wild, and manna dew;
And sure in language strange she said,
   I love thee true –

She took me to her elfin grot,
   And there she gazed and sighed full sore,
And there I shut her wild, wild eyes
   With kisses four.

And there she lullèd me asleep,
   And there I dream'd, ah woe betide,
The latest dream I ever dreamed
   On the cold hill side.

I saw pale kings, and princes too,
   Pale warriors, death-pale were they all;
Who cried – 'La belle Dame sans merci
   Hath thee in thrall!'

I saw their starv'd lips in the gloam
   With horrid warning gaped wide,
And I awoke, and found me here
   On the cold hill side.

And this is why I sojourn here
   Alone and palely loitering,
Though the sedge is withered from the lake,
   And no birds sing.

John Keats (1795–1821)

The Song of Hiawatha (extract)

By the shores of Gitche Gumee,
By the shining Big-Sea-Water,
Stood the wigwam of Nokomis,
Daughter of the Moon, Nokomis.
Dark behind it rose the forest,
Rose the black and gloomy pine-trees,
Rose the firs with cones upon them;
Bright before it beat the water,
Beat the clear and sunny water,
Beat the shining Big-Sea-Water.
There the wrinkled, old Nokomis
Nursed the little Hiawatha,
Rocked him in his linden cradle,
Bedded soft in moss and rushes,
Safely bound with reindeer sinews;
Stilled his fretful wail by saying,
"Hush! the Naked Bear will get thee!"
Lulled him into slumber, singing,
"Ewa-yea! my little owlet!
Who is this that lights the wigwam?
With his great eyes lights the wigwam?
Ewa-yea! my little owlet!"
Many things Nokomis taught him
Of the stars that shine in heaven;
Showed him Ishkoodah, the comet,
Ishkoodah, with fiery tresses;
Showed the Death-Dance of the spirits,
Warriors with their plumes and
    war-clubs,
Flaring far away to northward
In the frosty nights of Winter;
Showed the broad, white road in heaven,
Pathway of the ghosts, the shadows,
Running straight across the heavens,
Crowded with the ghosts, the shadows.
At the door on summer evenings
Sat the little Hiawatha;
Heard the whispering of pine-trees,
Heard the lapping of the water,
Sounds of music, words of wonder;
"Minne-wawa!" said the pine-trees,
"Mudway-aushka!" said the water.
Saw the firefly, Wah-wah-taysee,
Flitting through the dusk of evening,
With the twinkle of its candle
Lighting up the brakes and brushes;
And he sang the song of children,
Sang the song Nokomis taught him:
"Wah-wah-taysee, little firefly,
Little, flitting, white-fire insect,
Little, dancing, white-fire creature,
Light me with your little candle,
Ere upon my bed I lay me,
Ere in sleep I close my eyelids!"
Saw the moon rise from the water
Rippling, rounding from the water,
Saw the flecks and shadows on it,
Whispered, "What is that, Nokomis?"
And the good Nokomis answered:
"Once a warrior, very angry,
Seized his grandmother, and threw her
Up into the sky at midnight;
Right against the moon he threw her;
'Tis her body that you see there."
Saw the rainbow in the heaven,
In the eastern sky the rainbow,
Whispered, "What is that, Nokomis?"
And the good Nokomis answered:
"'Tis the heaven of flowers you see there;
All the wild-flowers of the forest,
All the lilies of the prairie,
When on earth they fade and perish,
Blossom in that heaven above us."
When he heard the owls at midnight,
Hooting, laughing in the forest,
"What is that?" he cried in terror;
"What is that," he said, "Nokomis?"
And the good Nokomis answered:
"That is but the owl and owlet,
Talking in their native language,
Talking, scolding at each other."
Then the little Hiawatha

Learned of every bird its language,
Learned their names and all their secrets,
How they built their nests in Summer,
Where they hid themselves in Winter,
Talked with them whene'er he met them,
Called them "Hiawatha's Chickens".
Of all beasts he learned the language,
Learned their names and all their secrets,
How the beavers built their lodges,
Where the squirrels hid their acorns,
How the reindeer ran so swiftly,
Why the rabbit was so timid,
Talked with them whene'er he met them,
Called them "Hiawatha's Brothers".

Henry Wadsworth Longfellow (1807–82)

The Sorrows of Werther

WERTHER had a love for Charlotte
Such as words could never utter;
Would you know how first he met her?
She was cutting bread and butter.

Charlotte was a married lady,
And a moral man was Werther,
And for all the wealth of Indies,
Would do nothing for to hurt her.

So he sighed and pined and ogled,
And his passion boiled and bubbled,
Till he blew his silly brains out,
And no more was by it troubled.

Charlotte, having seen his body
Borne before her on a shutter,
Like a well-conducted person,
Went on cutting bread and butter.

William Makepeace Thackeray (1811–1863)

Porphyria's Lover

The rain set early in to-night,
    The sullen wind was soon awake,
It tore the elm-tops down for spite,
    And did its worst to vex the lake:
    I listened with heart fit to break.
When glided in Porphyria; straight
    She shut the cold out and the storm,
And kneeled and made the cheerless grate
    Blaze up, and all the cottage warm;
    Which done, she rose, and from her form
Withdrew the dripping cloak and shawl,
    And laid her soiled gloves by, untied
Her hat and let the damp hair fall,
    And, last, she sat down by my side
    And called me. When no voice replied,
She put my arm about her waist,
    And made her smooth white shoulder bare,
And all her yellow hair displaced,
    And, stooping, made my cheek lie there,
    And spread o'er all her yellow hair,
Murmuring how she loved me – she
    Too weak, for all her heart's endeavour,
To set its struggling passion free
    From pride, and vainer ties dissever,
    And give herself to me for ever.
But passion sometimes would prevail,
    Nor could to-night's gay feast restrain
A sudden thought of one so pale
    For love of her, and all in vain:
    So, she was come through wind and rain.
Be sure I looked up at her eyes
    Happy and proud; at last I knew
Porphyria worshipped me; surprise
    Made my heart swell, and still it grew
    While I debated what to do.
That moment she was mine, mine, fair,
    Perfectly pure and good: I found
A thing to do, and all her hair
    In one long yellow string I wound
    Three times her little throat around,
And strangled her. No pain felt she;
    I am quite sure she felt no pain.
As a shut bud that holds a bee,
    I warily opened her lids; again
    Laughed the blue eyes without a stain.
And I untightened next the tress
    About her neck; her cheek once more
Blushed bright beneath my burning kiss:
    I propped her head up as before,
    Only, this time my shoulder bore
Her head, which droops upon it still:
    The smiling rosy little head,
So glad it has its utmost will,
    That all it scorned at once is fled,
    And I, its love, am gained instead!
Porphyria's love: she guessed not how
    Her darling one wish would be heard.
And thus we sit together now,
    And all night long we have not stirred,
    And yet God has not said a word!

Robert Browning (1812–1899)

Morte d'Arthur (extracts)

Arthur and his Knights of the Round Table are embroiled in a desperate struggle.

So all day long the noise of battle roll'd
Among the mountains by the winter sea;
Until King Arthur's table, man by man,
Had fallen in Lyonnesse about their Lord,
King Arthur: then, because his wound was deep,
The bold Sir Bedivere uplifted him,
Sir Bedivere, the last of all his knights,
And bore him to a chapel nigh the field,
A broken chancel with a broken cross,
That stood on a dark strait of barren land.
On one side lay the Ocean, and on one
Lay a great water, and the moon was full,
   Then spake King Arthur to Sir Bedivere:
'The sequel of to-day unsolders all
The goodliest fellowship of famous knights
Whereof this world holds record. Such a sleep
They sleep – the men I loved. I think that we
Shall never more, at any future time,
Delight our souls with talk of knightly deeds,
Walking about the gardens and the halls
Of Camelot, as in the days that were.
I perish by this people which I made, –
Tho' Merlin sware that I should come again
To rule once more – but let what will be, be,
I am so deeply smitten thro' the helm
That without help I cannot last till morn.
Thou therefore take my brand Excalibur,
Which was my pride: for thou rememberest how
In those old days, one summer noon, an arm
Rose up from out the bosom of the lake,
Clothed in white samite, mystic, wonderful,
Holding the sword – and how I row'd across
And took it, and have worn it, like a king:
And, wheresoever I am sung or told
In aftertime, this also shall be known:

But now delay not: take Excalibur,
And fling him far into the middle mere:
Watch what thou seëst, and lightly bring me word.'
   To him replied the bold Sir Bedivere:
'It is not meet, Sir King, to leave thee thus,
Aidless, alone, and smitten thro' the helm.
A little thing may harm a wounded man,
Yet I thy hest will all perform at full,
Watch what I see, and lightly bring thee word.'
   So saying, from the ruin'd shrine he stept
And in the moon athwart the place of tombs,
Where lay the mighty bones of ancient men,
Old knights, and over them the sea-wind sang
Shrill, chill, with flakes of foam. He, stepping down
By zig-zag paths, and juts of pointed rock,
Came on the shining levels of the lake.
   There drew he forth the brand Excalibur,
And o'er him, drawing it, the winter moon,
Brightening the skirts of a long cloud, ran forth
And sparkled keen with frost against the hilt:
For all the haft twinkled with diamond sparks,
Myriads of topaz-lights, and jacinth-work
Of subtlest jewellery. He gazed so long
That both his eyes were dazzled, as he stood,
This way and that dividing the swift mind,
In act to throw: but at the last it seem'd
Better to leave Excalibur conceal'd
There in the many-knotted waterflags,
That whistled stiff and dry about the marge.
So strode he back slow to the wounded King.
   Then spake King Arthur to Sir Bedivere:
'Hast thou perform'd my mission which I gave?
What is it thou hast seen? or what hast heard?'
And answer made the bold Sir Bedivere;
'I heard the ripple washing in the reeds,
And the wild water lapping on the crag.'
   To whom replied King Arthur, faint and pale:

'Thou hast betray'd thy nature and thy name,
Not rendering true answer, as beseem'd
Thy fealty, nor like a noble knight:
For surer sign had follow'd, either hand,
Or voice, or else a motion of the mere.
This is a shameful thing for men to lie.

Twice more Sir Bedivere is sent to throw the sword into the middle of the lake. The third time, fearful of Arthur's anger, he does so:

                                    The great brand
Made lightnings in the splendour of the moon,
And flashing round and round, and whirl'd in an arch,
Shot like a streamer of the northern morn,
Seen where the moving isles of winter shock
By night, with noises of the northern sea.
So flash'd and fell the brand Excalibur:
But ere he dipt the surface, rose an arm
Clothed in white samite, mystic, wonderful,
And caught him by the hilt, and brandish'd him
Three times, and drew him under in the mere.
And lightly went the other to the King.

When Bedivere reports what he saw to Arthur, the King knows that he is speaking the truth:

  And answer made King Arthur, breathing hard.
'My end draws nigh; 'tis time that I were gone.
Make broad thy shoulders to receive my weight,
And bear me to the margin; yet I fear
My wound hath taken cold, and I shall die.'

Narratives

And so Bedivere carries the dying Arthur to the lakeside.

  Then saw they how there hove a dusky barge,
Dark as a funeral scarf from stem to stern,
Beneath them; and descending they were ware
That all the decks were dense with stately forms
Black-stoled, black-hooded, like a dream – by these
Three Queens with crowns of gold – and from them
 rose
A cry that shiver'd to the tingling stars,
And, as it were one voice an agony
Of lamentation, like a wind, that shrills
All night in a waste land, where no one comes,
Or hath come, since the making of the world.
  Then murmur'd Arthur, 'Place me in the barge,'
And to the barge they came.

The three Queens weep at the sight of Arthur, lying like a shattered column:

Not like that Arthur who, with lance in rest,
From spur to plume a star of tournament,
Shot thro' the lists at Camelot, and charged
Before the eyes of ladies and of kings.

  Then loudly cried the bold Sir Bedivere,
'Ah! my Lord Arthur, whither shall I go?
Where shall I hide my forehead and my eyes?
For now I see the true old times are dead,
When every morning brought a noble chance,
And every chance brought out a noble knight.
Such times have not been since the light that led
The holy Elders with the gift of myrrh.
But now the whole Round Table is dissolved
Which was an image of the mighty world;
And I, the last, go forth companionless,
And the days darken round me, and the years,
Among new men, strange faces, other minds.'

    And slowly answered Arthur from the barge:
'The old order changeth, yielding place to new,
And God fulfils Himself in many ways,
Lest one good custom should corrupt the world.
Comfort thyself: what comfort is in me?
I have lived my life, and that which I have done
May He within Himself make pure! but thou,
If thou shouldst never see my face again,
Pray for my soul. More things are wrought by prayer
Than this world dreams of. Wherefore, let thy voice
Rise like a fountain for me night and day.
For what are men better than sheep or goats
That nourish a blind life within the brain,
If, knowing God, they lift not hands of prayer
Both for themselves and those who call them friend?
For so the whole round earth is every way
Bound by gold chains about the feet of God.
But now farewell. I am going a long way
With these thou seest – if indeed I go –
(For all my mind is clouded with a doubt)
To the island-valley of Avilion;
Where falls not hail, or rain, or any snow,
Nor ever wind blows loudly; but it lies
Deep-meadow'd, happy, fair with orchard-lawns
And bowery hollows crown'd with summer sea,
Where I will heal me of my grievous wound.'
    So said he, and the barge with oar and sail
Moved from the brink, like some full-breasted swan
That, fluting a wild carol ere her death,
Ruffles her pure cold plume, and takes the flood
With swarthy webs. Long stood Sir Bedivere
Revolving many memories, till the hull
Look'd one black dot against the verge of dawn,
And on the mere the wailing died away.

Alfred, Lord Tennyson (1809–1892)

The Lady Of Shalott

PART I

On either side the river lie
Long fields of barley and of rye,
That clothe the wold and meet the sky;
And thro' the field the road runs by
    To many-tower'd Camelot;
And up and down the people go,
Gazing where the lilies blow
Round an island there below,
    The island of Shalott.

Willows whiten, aspens quiver,
Little breezes dusk and shiver
Thro' the wave that runs for ever
By the island in the river
    Flowing down to Camelot.
Four grey walls, and four grey towers,
Overlook a space of flowers,
And the silent isle embowers
    The Lady of Shalott.

By the margin, willow-veil'd,
Slide the heavy barges trail'd
By slow horses; and unhail'd
The shallop flitteth silken-sail'd
    Skimming down to Camelot:
But who hath seen her wave her hand?
Or at the casement seen her stand?
Or is she known in all the land,
    The Lady of Shalott?

Only reapers, reaping early
In among the bearded barley,
Hear a song that echoes cheerly
From the river winding clearly,
    Down to tower'd Camelot:
And by the moon the reaper weary,
Piling sheaves in uplands airy,
Listening, whispers, ''Tis the fairy
    Lady of Shalott.'

PART II

There she weaves by night and day
A magic web with colours gay.
She has heard a whisper say,
A curse is on her if she stay
    To look down to Camelot.
She knows not what the curse may be,
And so she weaveth steadily,
And little other care hath she,
    The Lady of Shalott.

And moving thro' a mirror clear
That hangs before her all the year,
Shadows of the world appear.
There she sees the highway near
    Winding down to Camelot:
There the river eddy whirls,
And there the surly village-churls,
And the red cloaks of market girls,
    Pass onward from Shalott.

Sometimes a troop of damsels glad,
An abbot on an ambling pad,
Sometimes a curly shepherd-lad,
Or long-hair'd page in crimson clad,
    Goes by to tower'd Camelot;
And sometimes thro' the mirror blue
The knights come riding two and two:
She hath no loyal knight and true,
    The Lady of Shalott.

But in her web she still delights
To weave the mirror's magic sights,
For often thro' the silent nights
A funeral, with plumes and lights,
    And music, went to Camelot:
Or when the moon was overhead,
Came two young lovers lately wed:
'I am half sick of shadows,' said
    The Lady of Shalott.

Part III

A bow-shot from her bower-eaves,
He rode between the barley-sheaves,
The sun came dazzling thro' the leaves,
And flamed upon the brazen greaves
   Of bold Sir Lancelot.
A red-cross knight for ever kneel'd
To a lady in his shield,
That sparkled on the yellow field,
   Beside remote Shalott.

The gemmy bridle glitter'd free,
Like to some branch of stars we see
Hung in the golden Galaxy.
The bridle bells rang merrily
   As he rode down to Camelot:
And from his blazon'd baldric slung
A mighty silver bugle hung,
And as he rode his armour rung,
   Beside remote Shalott.

All in the blue unclouded weather
Thick-jewell'd shone the saddle-leather,
The helmet and the helmet-feather
Burn'd like one burning flame together,
   As he rode down to Camelot.
As often thro' the purple night,
Below the starry clusters bright,
Some bearded meteor, trailing light,
   Moves over still Shalott.

His broad clear brow in the sunlight glow'd;
On burnish'd hooves his war-horse trode;
From underneath his helmet flow'd
His coal-black curls as on he rode,
   As he rode down to Camelot.
From the bank and from the river
He flash'd into the crystal mirror,
'Tirra lirra,' by the river
   Sang Sir Lancelot.

She left the web, she left the loom,
She made three paces thro' the room,
She saw the water-lily bloom,
She saw the helmet and the plume,
   She look'd down to Camelot.
Out flew the web and floated wide;
The mirror crack'd from side to side;
'The curse is come upon me,' cried
   The Lady of Shalott.

Part IV

In the stormy east-wind straining,
The pale yellow woods were waning,
The broad stream in his banks complaining,
Heavily the low sky raining
   Over tower'd Camelot;
Down she came and found a boat
Beneath a willow left afloat,
And round about the prow she wrote
   The Lady of Shalott.

And down the river's dim expanse–
Like some bold seer in a trance,
Seeing all his own mischance–
With a glassy countenance
   Did she look to Camelot.
And at the closing of the day
She loosed the chain, and down she lay;
The broad stream bore her far away,
   The Lady of Shalott.

Lying, robed in snowy white
That loosely flew to left and right–
The leaves upon her falling light–
Thro' the noises of the night
   She floated down to Camelot:
And as the boat-head wound along
The willowy hills and fields among,
They heard her singing her last song,
   The Lady of Shalott.

Heard a carol, mournful, holy,
Chanted loudly, chanted lowly,
Till her blood was frozen slowly,
And her eyes were darken'd wholly,
   Turn'd to tower'd Camelot.
For ere she reach'd upon the tide
The first house by the water-side,
Singing in her song she died,
   The Lady of Shalott.

Under tower and balcony,
By garden-wall and gallery,
A gleaming shape she floated by,
Dead-pale between the houses high,
   Silent into Camelot.
Out upon the wharfs they came,
Knight and burgher, lord and dame,
And round the prow they read her name,
   The Lady of Shalott.

Who is this? And what is here?
And in the lighted palace near
Died the sound of royal cheer;
And they cross'd themselves for fear,
   All the knights at Camelot;
But Lancelot mused a little space;
He said, 'She has a lovely face;
God in His mercy lend her grace,
   The Lady of Shalott.'

Alfred, Lord Tennyson

How They Brought the Good News from Ghent to Aix

I sprang to the stirrup, and Joris, and he;
I galloped, Dirck galloped, we galloped all three;
"Good speed!" cried the watch, as the gate-bolts undrew;
"Speed!" echoed the wall to us galloping through;
Behind shut the postern, the lights sank to rest,
And into the midnight we galloped abreast.

Not a word to each other; we kept the great pace
Neck by neck, stride by stride, never changing our place;
I turned in my saddle and made its girths tight,
Then shortened each stirrup, and set the pique right,
Rebuckled the cheek-strap, chained slacker the bit,
Nor galloped less steadily Roland a whit.

'Twas moonset at starting; but while we drew near
Lokeren, the cocks crew and twilight dawned clear;
At Boom, a great yellow star came out to see;
At Düffeld, 'twas morning as plain as could be;
And from Mechlen church-steeple we heard the half-chime,
So Joris broke silence with, "Yet there is time!"

At Aerschot, up leaped of a sudden the sun,
And against him the cattle stood black every one,
To stare thro' the mist at us galloping past,
And I saw my stout galloper Roland at last,
With resolute shoulders, each butting away
The haze, as some bluff river headland its spray,

And his low head and crest, just one sharp ear bent back
For my voice, and the other pricked out on his track;
And one eye's black intelligence,– ever that glance
O'er its white edge at me, his own master, askance!
And the thick heavy spume-flakes which aye and anon
His fierce lips shook upwards in galloping on.

By Hasselt, Dirck groaned; and cried Joris, "Stay spur!
Your Roos galloped bravely, the fault's not in her,
We'll remember at Aix" – for one heard the quick wheeze
Of her chest, saw the stretched neck and staggering knees,
And sunk tail, and horrible heave of the flank,
As down on her haunches she shuddered and sank.

So we were left galloping, Joris and I,
Past Looz and past Tongres, no cloud in the sky;
The broad sun above laughed a pitiless laugh,
'Neath our feet broke the brittle bright stubble like chaff;
Till over by Dalhem a dome-spire sprang white,
And "Gallop," gasped Joris, "for Aix is in sight!

"How they'll greet us!" and all in a moment his roan
Rolled neck and croup over, lay dead as a stone;
And there was my Roland to bear the whole weight
Of the news which alone could save Aix from her fate,
With his nostrils like pits full of blood to the brim,
And with circles of red for his eye-socket's rim.

Then I cast loose my buffcoat, each holster let fall,
Shook off both my jack-boots, let go belt and all,
Stood up in the stirrup, leaned, patted his ear,
Called my Roland his pet-name, my horse without peer;
Clapped my hands, laughed and sang, any noise, bad or good,
Till at length into Aix Roland galloped and stood.

And all I remember is, friends flocking round
As I sate with his head 'twixt my knees on the ground,
And no voice but was praising this Roland of mine,
As I poured down his throat our last measure of wine,
Which (the burgesses voted by common consent)
Was no more than his due who brought good news from Ghent.

Robert Browning (1812–1889)

She was Poor but she was Honest

She was poor but she was honest,
   Victim of a rich man's game;
First he loved her, then he left her,
   And she lost her maiden name.

Then she hastened up to London,
   For to hide her grief and shame;
There she met another rich man,
   And she lost her name again.

See her riding in her carriage,
   In the Park and all so gay;
All the nibs and nobby persons
   Come to pass the time of day.

See them at the gay theáter
   Sitting in the costly stalls;
With one hand she holds the programme,
   With the other strokes his hand.

See him have her dance in Paris
   In her frilly underclothes;
All those Frenchies there applauding
   When she strikes a striking pose.

See the little country village
   Where her aged parents live;
Though they drink champagne she sends them,
   Still they never can forgive.

In the rich man's arms she flutters
   Like a bird with broken wing;
First he loved her, then he left her,
   And she hasn't got a ring.

See him in his splendid mansion
   Entertaining with the best,
While the girl as he has ruined
   Entertains a sordid guest.

See him riding in his carriage
   Past the gutter where she stands;
He has made a stylish marriage
   While she wrings her ringless hands.

See him in the House of Commons
   Passing laws to put down crime,
While the victim of his passions
   Slinks away to hide her shame.

See her on the bridge at midnight
   Crying, 'Farewell, faithless love!'
There's a scream, a splash – Good Heavens!
   What is she a-doing of?

Then they dragged her from the river,
   Water from her clothes they wrung;
They all thought that she was drownded,
   But the corpse got up and sung:

'It's the same the whole world over;
   It's the poor as gets the blame,
It's the rich as gets the pleasure –
   Ain't it all a bleeding shame!'

Unknown (19th Century)

(opposite) 'A City Thoroughfare', Gustave Doré, 1871

Songs

Adam Lay Ybounden

Adam lay ybounden
  Bounden in a bond;
Four thousand winter
  Thought he not too long.
And all was for an apple,
  An apple that he took,
As clerkës finden written
  In their book.
Nor had the apple taken been,
  The apple taken been,
Then had never our Lady
  A-been heaven's queen.
Blessed be the time
  That apple taken was!
Therefore we may singen
  Deo gracias!

Unknown

I Sing of a Maiden

I sing of a maiden
  That is makeless;*
King of all kings
  To her son she ches.*

He came all so still,
  There his mother was,
As dew in April
  That falleth on the grass.

He came all so still
  To his mother's bower,
As dew in April
  That falleth on the flower.

He came all so still –
  There his mother lay,
As dew in April
  That falleth on the spray.

Mother and maiden
  Was never none but she;
Well may such a lady
  God's mother be.

Unknown

---

* makeless – matchless
* ches – choose

A Psalm of David

The Lord is my shepherd; I shall not want.

He maketh me to lie down in green pastures: he leadeth me beside the still waters.

He restoreth my soul: he leadeth me in the paths of righteousness for his name's sake.

Yea, though I walk through the valley of the shadow of death, I will fear no evil: for thou art with me; thy rod and thy staff they comfort me.

Thou preparest a table before me in the presence of mine enemies: thou anointest my head with oil; my cup runneth over.

Surely goodness and mercy shall follow me all the days of my life: and I will dwell in the house of the Lord for ever.

From The Book of Psalms, *Psalm 23 (Authorised King James Version)*

'The man upright of life'

The man upright of life,
   Whose guiltless heart is free
From all dishonest deeds
   Or thought of vanity:

That man whose silent days
   In harmless joys are spent,
Whom hopes cannot delude
   Nor sorrows discontent:

That man needs neither towers
   Nor armour for defence,
Nor secret vaults to fly
   From thunder's violence.

He only can behold
   With unaffrighted eyes
The horrors of the deep
   And terrors of the skies.

Thus scorning all the cares
   That fate or fortune brings,
He makes his heaven his book,
   His wisdom heavenly things.

Good thoughts his only friends,
   His wealth a well-spent age,
The earth his sober inn
   And quiet pilgrimage.

Thomas Campion (1567–1620)

'Jack and Joan they think no ill'

Jack and Joan they think no ill,
But loving live, and merry still;
Do their weekdays' work, and pray
Devoutly on the holy day:
Skip and trip it on the green,
And help to choose the Summer Queen.
Lash out at a country feast
Their silver penny with the best.

Well can they judge of nappy* ale,
And tell at large a winter tale.
Climb up to the apple loft,
And turn the crabs till they be soft.
Tib is all the father's joy,
And little Tom the mother's boy,
All their pleasure is content,
And care to pay their yearly rent.

Joan can call by name her cows,
And deck her windows with green boughs.
She can wreaths and tutties make,
And trim with plums a bridal cake.
Jack knows what brings gain or loss,
And his long flail can stoutly toss;
Make the hedge which others break,
And ever thinks what he doth speak.

Now you courtly dames and knights,
That study only strange delights,
Though you scorn the home-spun grey
And revel in your rich array,
Though your tongues dissemble deep
And can your heads from danger keep,
Yet for all your pomp and train,
Securer lives the silly swain.

Thomas Campion

* nappy: foaming, strong

'Beauty sat bathing by a spring'

Beauty sat bathing by a spring
  Where fairest shades did hide her.
The winds blew calm, the birds did sing,
  The cool streams ran beside her.
My wanton thoughts enticed mine eye
  To see what was forbidden,
But better memory said, fie.
  So vain desire was chidden.
    Hey nonny no, nonny nonny.

Into a slumber then I fell,
  When fond imagination
Seemed to see, but could not tell
  Her feature or her fashion.
But even as babes in dreams do smile,
  And sometime fall a-weeping,
So I awaked as wise this while
  As when I fell a-sleeping.
    Hey nonny no, nonny nonny.

Anthony Munday (1560–1633)

'Since your sweet cherry lips I kissed'

Since your sweet cherry lips I kissed,
No want of food I once have missed;
My stomach now no meat requires,
My throat no drink at all desires;
For by your breath, which then I gained,
Chameleon-like my life's maintained.

Then grant me, dear, those cherries still,
O let me feed on them my fill;
If by a surfeit death I get,
Upon my tomb let this be set:
Here lieth he whom cherries two
Made both to live and life forgo.

Francis Davison (?1575–1619)

'Love in thy youth, fair maid'

Love in thy youth, fair maid. Be wise.
  Old Time will make thee colder.
And though each morning new arise,
  Yet we each day grow older.

Thou as heaven art fair and young,
  Thine eyes like twin stars shining.
But ere another day be sprung,
  All these will be declining.

Then Winter comes with all his fears,
  And all thy sweets shall borrow.
Too late then wilt thou shower thy tears,
  And I too late shall sorrow.

Walter Porter (16th/17th century)

'Look on me ever'

Look on me ever, though thine eye
  Murder where it glances.
If by so happy means I die,
  My fortune it advances.
And if by chance a tear you shed
  To show my death did move you,
It will revive me being dead,
  And I again shall love you.
Redeem me from so deep despair;
  The power you have, now try it.
Think me but fair, and I am fair,
  Although the world deny it.

Walter Porter

'Gather ye rose-buds while ye may'

GATHER ye rose-buds while ye may,
   Old Time is still a-flying:
And this same flower that smiles to-day,
   To-morrow will be dying.

The glorious Lamp of Heaven, the Sun,
   The higher he's a-getting
The sooner will his race be run,
   And nearer he's to setting.

That age is best which is the first,
   When youth and blood are warmer;
But being spent, the worse, and worst
   Times, still succeed the former.

Then, be not coy, but use your time;
   And while ye may, go marry:
For having lost but once your prime,
   You may for ever tarry.

Robert Herrick (1591–1674)

'Cherry ripe'

CHERRY ripe, ripe, ripe, I cry,
   Full and fair ones; come and buy:
If so be, you ask me where
They do grow? I answer, 'There,
Where my Julia's lips do smile
There's the land, or Cherry Isle:
Whose plantations fully show
All the year, where Cherries grow.'

Robert Herrick

The Song of Master Valiant-for-Truth

Who would true valour see,
  Let him come hither;
One here will constant be,
  Come wind, come weather.
There's no discouragement
Shall make him once relent
His first avow'd intent
  To be a pilgrim.

Whoso beset him round,
  With dismal stories,
Do but themselves confound;
  His strength the more is.
No lion can him fright,
He'll with a giant fight,
But he will have a right
  To be a pilgrim.

Hobgoblin, nor foul fiend,
  Can daunt his spirit:
He knows, he at the end
  Shall Life inherit.
Then fancies fly away,
He'll fear not what men say,
He'll labour night and day
  To be a pilgrim.

John Bunyan (1628–1688)

The Shepherd Boy's Song

He that is down, needs fear no fall,
He that is low, no pride;
He that is humble, ever shall
   Have God to be his guide.

I am content with what I have,
   Little be it, or much:
And, Lord, contentment still I crave,
   Because thou savest such.

Fullness to such a burden is
   That go on pilgrimage:
Here little, and hereafter bliss
   Is best from age to age.

John Bunyan

'When icicles hang by the wall'

When icicles hang by the wall,
   And Dick the shepherd blows his nail,
And Tom bears logs into the hall,
   And milk comes frozen home in pail,
When blood is nipp'd and ways be foul,
Then nightly sings the staring owl,
   Tu-whit;
Tu-who, a merry note,
While greasy Joan doth keel* the pot.

When all aloud the wind doth blow,
   And coughing drowns the parson's saw,*
And birds sit brooding in the snow,
   And Marion's nose looks red and raw,
When roasted crabs hiss in the bowl,
Then nightly sings the staring owl,
   Tu-whit;
Tu-who, a merry note,
While greasy Joan doth keel the pot.

William Shakespeare (1564–1616)

* keel: stir   * saw: discourse, sermon

'Fear no more the heat o' the sun'

Fear no more the heat o' the sun,
   Nor the furious winter's rages;
Thou thy worldly task hast done,
   Home art gone, and ta'en thy wages;
Golden lads and girls all must
   As chimney-sweepers, come to dust.

Fear no more the frown o' the great,
   Thou art past the tyrant's stroke:
Care no more to clothe and eat;
   To thee the reed is as the oak;
The sceptre, learning, physic, must
   All follow this, and come to dust.

Fear no more the lightning-flash,
   Nor the all-dreaded thunder-stone;
Fear not slander, censure rash;
   Thou hast finish'd joy and moan:
All lovers young, all lovers must
   Consign to thee, and come to dust.

No exorciser harm thee!
   Nor no witchcraft charm thee!
Ghost unlaid forbear thee!
   Nothing ill come near thee!
Quiet consummation have;
   And renowned be thy grave!

William Shakespeare

Sally in our Alley

Of all the girls that are so smart
   There's none like pretty Sally;
She is the darling of my heart,
   And she lives in our alley.
There is no lady in the land
   Is half so sweet as Sally;
She is the darling of my heart,
   And she lives in our alley.

Her father he makes cabbage-nets,
   And through the streets does cry 'em;
Her mother she sells laces long
   To such as please to buy 'em:
But sure such folks could ne'er beget
   So sweet a girl as Sally!
She is the darling of my heart,
   And she lives in our alley.

When she is by, I leave my work,
   I love her so sincerely;
My master comes like any Turk,
   And bangs me most severely:
But let him bang his bellyful,
   I'll bear it all for Sally;
She is the darling of my heart,
   And she lives in our alley.

Of all the days that's in the week
   I dearly love but one day –
And that's the day that comes betwixt
   A Saturday and Monday;
For then I'm dressed all in my best
   To walk abroad with Sally;
She is the darling of my heart,
   And she lives in our alley.

My master carries me to church,
   And often am I blamèd
Because I leave him in the lurch
   As soon as text is namèd;
I leave the church in sermon-time
   And slink away to Sally;
She is the darling of my heart,
   And she lives in our alley.

When Christmas comes about again,
   O, then I shall have money;
I'll hoard it up, and box it all,
   I'll give it to my honey:
I would it were ten thousand pound,
   I'd give it all to Sally;
She is the darling of my heart,
   And she lives in our alley.

My master and the neighbours all
   Make game of me and Sally,
And, but for her, I'd better be
   A slave and row a galley;
But when my seven long years are out,
   O, then I'll marry Sally;
O, then we'll wed, and then we'll bed –
   But not in our alley!

Henry Carey (?1687–1743)

The Sluggard

'Tis the voice of the sluggard; I heard him complain,
 "You have waked me too soon, I must slumber again."
As the door on its hinges, so he on his bed,
Turns his sides, and his shoulders, and his heavy head.

"A little more sleep, and a little more slumber;"
Thus he wastes half his days and his hours without number,
And when he gets up, he sits folding his hands,
Or walks about sauntering, or trifling he stands.

I pass'd by his garden, and saw the wild brier,
The thorn and the thistle, grow broader and higher;
The clothes that hang on him are turning to rags;
And his money still wastes, till he starves, or he begs.

I made him a visit, still hoping to find
He had took better care for improving his mind:
He told me his dreams, talk'd of eating and drinking,
But he scarce reads his Bible, and never loves thinking.

Said I then to my heart, "Here's a lesson for me;
That man's but a picture of what I might be;
But thanks to my friends for their care in my breeding,
Who taught me betimes to love working and reading."

Isaac Watts (1674–1748)

'No riches from his scanty store'

No riches from his scanty store
  My lover could impart;
He gave a boon I valued more –
  He gave me all his heart!

His soul sincere, his generous worth,
  Might well this bosom move;
And when I asked for bliss on earth,
  I only meant his love.

But now for me, in search of gain
  From shore to shore he flies;
Why wander riches to obtain,
  When love is all I prize?

The frugal meal, the lowly cot
  If blest my love with thee!
That simple fare, that humble lot,
  Were more than wealth to me.

While he the dangerous ocean braves,
  My tears but vainly flow:
Is pity in the faithless waves
  To which I pour my woe?

The night is dark, the waters deep,
  Yet soft the billows roll;
Alas! at every breeze I weep –
  The storm is in my soul.

Helen Maria Williams (1762–1827)

Ye banks and braes

Ye banks and braes o' bonnie Doon
   How can ye blume sae fair!
How can ye chant, ye little birds,
   And I sae fu' o' care!

Thou'll break my heart, thou bonnie bird
   That sings upon the bough;
Thou minds me o' the happy days
   When my fause Luve was true.

Thou'll break my heart, thou bonnie bird
   That sings beside thy mate;
For sae I sat, and sae I sang,
   And wist na o' my fate.

Aft hae I roved by bonnie Doon
   To see the woodbine twine,
And ilka bird sang o' its love;
   And sae did I o' mine.

Wi' lightsome heart I pu'd a rose,
   Frae aff its thorny tree;
And my fause luver staw the rose,
   But left the thorn wi' me.

Robert Burns (1759–1796)

A red, red rose

Oh, my luve's like a red, red rose,
   That's newly sprung in June;
Oh, my luve's like the melodie
   That's sweetly played in tune.

As fair art thou, my bonnie lass,
   So deep in luve am I;
And I will luve thee still, my dear,
   Till a' the seas gang dry.

Till a' the seas gang dry, my dear,
   And the rocks melt wi' the sun:
I will luve thee still, my dear,
   While the sands o' life shall run.

And fare thee weel, my only luve!
   And fare thee weel a while!
And I will come again, my luve,
   Though it were ten thousand mile.

Robert Burns

The War Song of Dinas Vawr

The mountain sheep are sweeter,
But the valley sheep are fatter;
We therefore deemed it meeter
To carry off the latter.
We made an expedition;
We met a host and quelled it;
We forced a strong position,
And killed the men who held it.

On Dyfed's richest valley,
Where herds of kine were browsing,
We made a mighty sally,
To furnish our carousing.
Fierce warriors rushed to meet us;
We met them, and o'erthrew them:
They struggled hard to beat us;
But we conquered them, and slew them.

As we drove our prize at leisure,
The king marched forth to catch us:
His rage surpassed all measure,
But his people could not match us.
He fled to his hall-pillars;
And, ere our force we led off,
Some sacked his house and cellars,
While others cut his head off.

We there, in strife bewildering,
Spilt blood enough to swim in:
We orphaned many children,
And widowed many women.
The eagles and the ravens
We glutted with our foemen:
The heroes and the cravens,
The spearmen and the bowmen.

We brought away from battle,
And much their land bemoaned them,
Two thousand head of cattle,
And the head of him who owned them:
Ednyfed, King of Dyfed,
His head was borne before us;
His wine and beasts supplied our feasts,
And his overthrow, our chorus.

Thomas Love Peacock (1785–1866)

'Yes, Mary Ann'

Yes, Mary Ann, I freely grant,
  The charms of Henry's eyes I see;
But while I gaze, I something want,
  I want those eyes – to gaze on me.

And I allow, in Henry's heart
  Not Envy's self a fault can see:
Yet still I must one wish impart,
  I wish that heart – to sigh for me.

Amelia Opie (1769–1853)

Caller Herrin'

Wha'll buy caller* herrin'?
They're bonnie fish and halesome farin';*
Wha'll buy caller herrin',
New drawn frae the Forth?

When ye were sleepin' on your pillows,
Dream'd ye aught o' our puir fellows,
Darkling as they faced the billows,
A' to fill the woven willows?

Wha'll buy my caller herrin'?
Oh, ye may ca' them vulgar farin',
Wives and mithers, maist despairing,
Ca' them lives o' men.

When the creel* o' herrin' passes,
Ladies, clad in silks and laces,
Gather in their braw pelisses,
Cast their heads and screw their faces,
   Wha'll buy caller herrin'?

Caller herrin's no to lightlie,
Ye can trip the spring fu' tightlie,*
Spite o' tauntin', flauntin', flingin',
Gow has set you a' a-singing,
   Wha'll buy caller herrin'?

Neibour wives, now tent my tellin':
When the bonny fish ye're sellin'
At a word aye be your dealin',
Truth will stand when a' thing's failin'.

Wha'll buy caller herrin'?
They're bonny fish and halesome farin':
Wha'll buy caller herrin',
New drawn frae the Forth?

Carolina Nairne (1766–1845)

* caller – fresh
* halesome farin' – wholesome food
* creel – basket
* tightlie – strenuously

'Sing me a song of a lad that is gone'

Sing me a song of a lad that is gone,
   Say, could that lad be I?
Merry of soul he sailed on a day
   Over the sea to Skye.

Mull was astern, Rum on the port,
   Eigg on the starboard bow;
Glory of youth glowed in his soul:
   Where is that glory now?

Sing me a song of a lad that is gone,
   Say, could that lad be I?
Merry of soul he sailed on a day
   Over the sea to Skye.

Give me again all that was there,
   Give me the sun that shone!
Give me the eyes, give me the soul,
   Give me the lad that's gone!

Sing me a song of a lad that is gone,
   Say, could that lad be I?
Merry of soul he sailed on a day
   Over the sea to Skye.

Billow and breeze, islands and seas,
   Mountains of rain and sun,
All that was good, all that was fair,
   All that was me is gone.

Robert Louis Stevenson (1850–1894)

Battle Hymn of the Republic

Mine eyes have seen the glory of the coming of the Lord;
He is trampling out the vintage where the grapes of wrath are stored;
He hath loosed the fatal lightning of his terrible swift sword:
   His Truth is marching on.

I have seen him in the watch-fires of a hundred circling camps;
They have builded him an altar in the evening dews and damps;
I have read his righteous sentence by the dim and flaring lamps:
   His Day is marching on.

I have read a fiery gospel, writ in burnished rows of steel:
'As you deal with my contemners, so with you my grace shall deal';
Let the Hero born of woman crush the serpent with his heel,
   Since God is marching on.

He has sounded forth the trumpet that shall never call retreat;
He is sifting out the hearts of men before his judgement-seat;
O be swift, my soul, to answer him; be jubilant, my feet!
   Our God is marching on.

In the beauty of the lilies Christ was born across the sea,
With a glory in his bosom that transfigures you and me;
As he died to make men holy, let us die to make men free,
   While God is marching on.

He is coming like the glory of the morning on the wave;
He is wisdom to the mighty, he is succour to the brave;
So the world shall be his footstool, and the soul of time his slave:
   Our God is marching on.

Julia Ward Howe (1819–1910)

A Nightmare

When you're lying awake with a dismal headache, and repose is taboo'd by anxiety,
I conceive you may use any language you choose to indulge in without impropriety;
For your brain is on fire – the bedclothes conspire of usual slumber to plunder you:
First your counterpane goes and uncovers your toes, and your sheet slips demurely from under you;
Then the blanketing tickles – you feel like mixed pickles, so terribly sharp is the pricking,
And you're hot, and you're cross, and you tumble and toss till there's nothing 'twixt you and the ticking.
Then the bedclothes all creep to the ground in a heap, and you pick 'em all up in a tangle;
Next your pillow resigns and politely declines to remain at its usual angle!
Well, you get some repose in the form of a doze, with hot eyeballs and head ever aching,
But your slumbering teems with such horrible dreams that you'd very much better be waking;
For you dream you are crossing the Channel, and tossing about in a steamer from Harwich,
Which is something between a large bathing-machine and a very small second-class carriage;
And you're giving a treat (penny ice and cold meat) to a party of friends and relations –
They're a ravenous horde – and they all came on board at Sloane Square and South Kensington Stations.
And bound on that journey you find your attorney (who started that morning from Devon);
He's a bit undersized, and you don't feel surprised when he tells you he's only eleven.
Well, you're driving like mad with this singular lad (by the bye the ship's now a four-wheeler),
And you're playing round games, and he calls you bad names when you tell him that 'ties pay the dealer';
But this you can't stand, so you throw up your hand, and you find you're as cold as an icicle,

In your shirt and your socks (the black silk with gold clocks), crossing Salisbury Plain on a bicycle:
And he and the crew are on bicycles too – which they've somehow or other invested in –
And he's telling the tars all the particu*lars* of a company he's interested in –
It's a scheme of devices, to get at low prices, all goods from cough mixtures to cables
(Which tickled the sailors) by treating retailers, as though they were all vege*ta*bles –
You get a good spadesman to plant a small tradesman (first take off his boots with a boot-tree),
And his legs will take root, and his fingers will shoot, and they'll blossom and bud like a fruit-tree –
From the greengrocer tree you get grapes and green pea, cauliflower, pineapple, and cranberries,
While the pastry-cook plant cherry-brandy will grant – apple puffs, and three-corners, and banberries –
The shares are a penny, and ever so many are taken by Rothschild and Baring,
And just as a few are allotted to you, you awake with a shudder despairing –
You're a regular wreck, with a crick in your neck, and no wonder you snore, for your head's on the floor, and you've needles and pins from your soles to your shins, and your flesh is a-creep, for your left leg's asleep, and you've cramp in your toes, and a fly on your nose, and some fluff in your lung, and a feverish tongue, and a thirst that's intense, and a general sense that you haven't been sleeping in clover;
But the darkness has passed, and it's daylight at last, and and the night has been long – ditto, ditto my song – and thank goodness they're both of them over!

W.S. Gilbert (1836–1911)

On Prince Frederick

Here lies Fred
Who was alive and is dead.
Had it been his father,
I had much rather;
Had it been his brother,
Still better than another;
Had it been his sister,
No one would have missed her;
Had it been the whole generation,
So much the better for the nation;
But since 'tis only Fred
Who was alive and is dead,
Why, there's no more to be said. *Unknown*

The Death of Huskisson

The trains are stopp'd, the MIGHTY CHIEFS OF FLAME
To quench their thirst the crystal water claim;
While from their post the great in crowds alight,
When, by a line-train, in its hasty flight,
Through striving to avoid it, Huskisson
By unforeseen mischance was over-run.
That stroke, alas! was death in shortest time;
Thus fell the great financier in his prime!
This fatal chance not only caused delay,
But damped the joy that erst had crown'd the day. *T. Baker*

On Peter Robinson

Here lies the preacher, judge, and poet, Peter
Who broke the laws of God, and man, and metre. *Lord Jeffrey*

Index of Authors

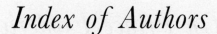

Arnold, Matthew 65
Baker, T. 151
Barron, W. R. J. 101
Behn, Aphra 53
Blake, William 56, 57
Brontë, Emily 64
Browning, Elizabeth Barrett 43
Browning, Robert 118, 127
Bunyan, John 138, 139
Burns, Robert 144
Byron, Lord George 30, 59
Campion, Thomas 133, 134
Carroll, Lewis 90, 92
Carey, Henry 141
Chaucer, Geoffrey 102, 104, 106, 108
Clough, Arthur Hugh 63
Coghill, Neville 103, 105, 107, 109
Coleridge, Samuel Taylor 110
Crabbe, George 112
Davison, Francis 135
Dickinson, Emily 67, 68
Donne, John 40, 41
Drayton, Michael 10
Elliot, Jane 28
Gilbert, W. S. 20, 149
Goldsmith, Oliver 27
Hemans, Felicia 31
Herrick, Robert 50, 137
Hoffman, Heinrich 85
Hood, Thomas 14, 61
Hopkins, Gerard Manley 69
Horsley, Henry Sharpe 81
Howe, Julia Ward 148
Hunt, James Henry Leigh 62
Jeffrey, Lord 151
Jones, Ernest 16
Keats, John 60, 115

Kipling, Rudyard 70
Lear, Edward 95
Longfellow, Henry Wadsworth 116
Lydgate, John William 74
MacGonagall, William 35
Martin, William 88
Marvell, Andrew 52
Mew, Charlotte 69
Meynell, Alice 44
Milton, John 41
Munday, Anthony 135
Nairne, Carolina 146
Opie, Amelia 145
Paterson, Banjo 23
Peacock, Thomas Love 145
Pope, Alexander 54
Porter, Walter 136
Raleigh, Walter 49
Richardson, Robert 98
Robinson, Mary 55
Rossetti, Christina 43, 44
Saxe, John Godfrey 89
Scott, Walter 15
Shakespeare, William 40, 139, 140
Shelley, Percy Bysshe 42
Shepherd, Nathaniel Graham 18
Shirley, James 51
Sidney, Philip 49
Stevenson, Robert Louis 147
Suckling, John 50
Tennyson, Lord Alfred 34, 119, 124
Thackeray, William Makepeace 117
Watkin, Sir Edward 37
Watts, Isaac 142
Whittier, John Greenleaf 32
Williams, Helen Maria 143
Wolfe, Charles 29
Wordsworth, William 12, 42, 58, 59